SCOTTISH
LEGAL SYSTEM

Law Essentials

SCOTTISH
LEGAL SYSTEM

2nd edition

Bryan Clark, B.A., LL.M., Ph.D.

Reader in Law, University of Strathclyde

DUNDEE UNIVERSITY PRESS
2009

First edition published in Great Britain in 2006 by
Dundee University Press
University of Dundee
Dundee DD1 4HN

www.dup.dundee.ac.uk

Reprinted 2007, 2008
Second edition published 2009

ISBN 978 1 84586 063 9

No natural forests were destroyed to make this product;
only farmed timber was used and replanted.

British Library Cataloguing-in-Publication Data
A catalogue record for this book is available on request from the British Library

Typeset by Waverley Typesetters, Fakenham, Norfolk
Printed and bound by Bell & Bain Ltd, Glasgow

CONTENTS

TABLE OF CASES

TABLE OF STATUTES

1 INTRODUCTION AND HISTORICAL DEVELOPMENT

To set Scots law in a wider context, it is worth noting at the outset that the Scottish legal system may be classified as "mixed". This classification stems from the fact that the Scottish legal system lies somewhere in between the two classic types of legal regime: "civil law" (or "civilian") and "common law" systems. Civil law systems are derived historically from Roman law and are commonplace in continental Europe. Common law systems, by contrast, are drawn from English law and are found in England as one might expect, and also in Commonwealth nations and many US states. The two schools may be distinguished on the basis that civil law systems are based upon legal deduction (ie rules deduced through general principles originally expounded by legal scholars), whereas common law systems are founded upon legal induction (ie the formation of legal principles induced through court decisions in particular instances).

It is appropriate to mention here that the terms "civil law" and "common law" are somewhat confusing in that they also hold other meanings (aside from those described above). The term "civil law" can also be used to denote law that, in general, regulates relations between private individuals in particular circumstances such as contract law, property law and delict (essentially, negligence law) as opposed to criminal law, whereby a minimum moral standard of behaviour is laid down by the state and prohibits particular activities, such as murder, rape, assault and theft, by their classification as criminal acts. Moreover, the term "common law" can be used to denote law which is non-statutory in nature – ie principles developed primarily through the courts and not borne out of legislation. Much of Scots law is rooted in common law principles (see Chapter 2).

In terms of other classifications, Scots law can also be split into public law and private law. Public law comprises those legal rules which relate specifically to the state. Public law examples include constitutional law and administrative law, which set out rules pertaining to the powers of the organs of the state and governing the ability of the state in all its forms to regulate the lives of the public. Private law covers law which does not pertain specifically to the state. This division between private and public law has long been recognised and has its roots in early Roman and Greek law. The division is not, however, clear-cut and some commentators have doubted its value, given that there is no essential difference between the respective sources of private and public law, nor the procedure or courts in which rights thereunder are determined.

In terms of schools of law, the legal system in Scotland is interesting in that it exhibits features of both the civil law (Roman) and common law (English) systems (although in its present form it probably leans more towards the common law model). The fact that the Scottish system is "mixed" in this way is no curious anomaly. Even a cursory analysis of the historical development of Scots law reveals significant influences from both sides of the legal school divide that have left an indelible imprint upon today's Scottish legal system. Indeed, our legal system has a rich and varied heritage and a somewhat colourful historical development. While a detailed exposition of the historical journey of the legal system in Scotland is beyond the scope of this short book, a summary of its evolution (highlighting some of the key influencing factors) is set out below.

HISTORICAL DEVELOPMENT

Early English (Norman) influence

The origins of any legal system typically coincide with the emergence of a nation. Scotland, as a nation, broadly emerged at the Battle of Carham in 1018 (or 1016), which in general brought together four separate tribes of peoples: the "Picts", arguably Scotland's indigenous peoples; the "Scots", in fact a tribe of Irish descent; the "Angles", a Germanic tribe brought in to the border provinces by the Romans to help stabilise the region; and the "Britons", a tribe which originally settled in the west of the land. While the incumbent laws of that time were largely customary and their development sporadic, the first major influence on the fledgling Scottish legal system occurred in the mid-11th century by way of English "feudalism" (in fact an idea imported to England by the Normans after the Battle of Hastings in 1066). The high watermark of English feudal influence occurred during the reign of King David I, who ruled in Scotland from 1124 to 1153. David had spent much of his early life in England and, being impressed by the system of governance that he found south of the border, he imported feudalism into Scotland as well as other early English legal institutions (such as the office of sheriff, which has endured to this day). Feudalism is essentially a system of landownership, the underlying fundamental premise of which is that all lands belong to the Crown (monarch). The Crown would grant or "feu" land to noblemen in return for "feu duties" which might include monetary payments, military allegiance and other forms of service. In turn, those in receipt of lands from the Crown ("Tenants in Chief") would then feu parts of that land to others known as "vassals", again in return for particular feu duties. The land could then be "sub-feued" again and split into yet smaller parcels, and hence what can be termed a "feudal pyramid" ensued with the monarch perched firmly at the top.

From this feudal structure developed not only a form of landownership but in fact a system of "top-down" societal governance and control. This dissemination of political power through feudalism was bolstered as the Tenants in Chief (or "Barons") developed courts on their lands within which they meted out justice and settled claims. A king's court was also set up to disseminate the monarch's power and sheriff courts were established to administer civil and criminal justice on behalf of the king across the land. The sheriff's role was overseen by "justiciars", officials who were imbued with extensive judicial powers in both criminal and civil matters. Over time the role of the justiciar fell into abeyance but their jurisdiction in criminal proceedings can be seen as a forerunner to the development of Scotland's supreme criminal court, the High Court of Justiciary, in 1672, which remains in place to this day.

Norse law

From as early as the middle of the 9th century, the land that was to become Scotland became subject to attacks from Scandinavian forces which were repeated over many centuries. Although Scotland was never conquered as such, the Viking raiders did establish settlements in western and northern areas such as the Hebridean Isles, Orkney and Shetland. These island areas began to be heavily influenced by Norse law and custom as a result. Some of this influence, most notably "udal law", the law pertaining to landownership, has survived into modern times.

Canon law

Aside from the courts described above, from the middle of the 12th century, the Canon law of the Roman Catholic Church began to exert its influence through Church courts dealing principally with family law and related matters, with decisions commonly reviewed in Rome. These courts continued to exercise jurisdiction up to the time of the reformation in 1559 when the Church's judicial functions were abolished in Scotland and any new influence of Canon law waned. Nevertheless, certain areas of Scots law (in particular, family law), to this day still bear the hallmarks of much of this early ecclesiastical influence.

Roman law

The historical influence of Roman law was felt at a later date and occurred in a number of ways. The infiltration of Roman law into Scotland began in the middle of the 16th century when, with scant opportunity for the study of law at Scottish universities, Scots law students travelled to France and, later, the Netherlands for legal instruction. Given that Roman law had been widely received across continental Europe at this time, on returning home and being faced with issues in which there were no applicable Scottish legal principles, Scots lawyers would naturally fall back on their Roman law learning to fill in the gaps.

Another key event in the influence of Roman law occurred in 1532 when the first permanent civil (ie non-criminal) court in Scotland, the Court of Session, was established. Based on a Roman model, the judiciary that manned this institution (which still endures to this day, albeit in a different form) was primarily educated in Roman and Canon law and hence the impact of these schools of legal thought was felt as the operation of the court developed.

As the court began to mature, so too legal writing became increasingly important. Beginning in the mid-17th century and continuing over the next 150 years or so, a substantial body of work was produced by eminent legal scholars known as "institutional writers". As will be noted in the next chapter, these seminal works became so revered and influential that they came to represent a valid source of law in themselves. They were thus instrumental in charting the development of Scots law as it moved into a more modern age. Many of these early jurists were schooled in Roman law and hence their work, although drawing upon a number of influencing factors, often bore the hallmarks of Roman law.

English law: the dominant modern influence

Although Roman principles continued to be expounded in institutional writings until the early 19th century, the beginning of the demise of Scotland's affinity with Roman law began with the Act of Union of 1707. A partnership borne largely out of political expediency rather than affection, the Act of Union brought about the amalgamation of the respective parliaments in Scotland and England. The Crowns of Scotland and England had already been amalgamated in 1606 when James VI of Scotland ascended the English throne as James I. A crisis arose when the last of the Stewart dynasty, Queen Anne, died without leaving an heir. Bitter disagreement between Scotland and England ensued as to who should ascend the throne.

Neither country was in a position to accept war as a viable option at that time: England was at war with France and Scotland was desperately impoverished and dependent upon continued trade links with its southern neighbour. Hence an agreement was reached between the two countries that Scotland would recognise Sophia of Hanover as successor to the throne and in return England would grant freedom of trade to the Scots. The treaty also entailed the Union of the two parliaments.

Despite mass protests on the streets of Scotland's cities, the incumbent Scottish Parliament which had developed as an offshoot of the Crown in the mid-15th century was abolished in tandem with its English counterpart and the new Parliament of Great Britain was established at Westminster. Although, under the Act of Union, Scotland was entitled to retain its own independent legal system and distinct Scottish laws (with the caveat that English revenue law would apply to Scotland), by virtue of the terms of the treaty, the laws of Scotland could in general be amended by any new legislation passed by the Westminster Parliament. Any new laws enacted at Westminster would automatically become binding upon the Scottish people and the Scottish courts and override any contrary Scottish common law (non-statutory) principles that had hitherto developed and any contrary Acts of the old Scottish Parliament. In addition, shortly after the Act of Union, the English-dominated House of Lords (sitting as a court) quickly assumed the role of hearing appeals on Scottish civil (non-criminal) matters from the Court of Session. These events laid the foundations for English law to become the predominant influencing factor over the next three centuries.

More specifically, as commerce and industry began to develop during the 18th century, Scotland began to turn towards and adopt English commercial and mercantile laws, which were much more mature than the incumbent Scottish equivalents. At the same time, the mass exodus by Scots lawyers to universities in continental Europe ceased at the time of the Napoleonic Wars in the early 1800s. Additionally, the Industrial Revolution in the 1850s led to increased parliamentary activism and the enactment of an unprecedented glut of statutory legislation to regulate increasingly complex social norms, working methods and technologies. The bulk of this new legislation often codified and built upon English common law principles and was extended across the whole of Britain, washing away many distinct Scots principles in the process.

Similarly, principles of Scots law began to dissipate in a number of areas as the heavy-handed influence of the House of Lords (sitting as a court) began to be felt when a series of Scottish civil (non-criminal) decisions in the Court of Session were overruled, arguably by the erroneous imposition of English doctrines.

Students of Scots law may quickly become aware of an antipathy that exists towards English law in certain Scottish legal circles, particularly in respect of the decimation of much of Scots law and its replacement with English principles since the Act of Union in 1707. Nevertheless, in the modern day, one should perhaps not lose sight of the fact that the origin of any particular law is not, in itself, of much import when compared to the quality of that legal principle. We should be proud of our legal heritage and be wary of the importation of inferior legal doctrines; but we might pose the question that if a law is crafted to be fair and reasonable, logical, efficient, enforceable in practice and to fulfil a societal need, should its historical origin be of any consequence?

The impact of the European Union

While English law can thus be considered the major modern influence on the development of Scottish law, more recent political events have brought to bear new impacts on the Scottish legal system. In particular, European Community law (EC law) has played a significant role since the UK joined the (then) European Economic Community (EEC) in 1973 and the European Communities Act 1972 was passed to give effect to EC law within the UK. The legislation and legislative process of the (now) European Union (EU) are discussed in Chapter 2 but suffice to say here that, to the disquiet of some commentators and to the glee of others, in the pursuit of the harmonisation of laws across EC Member States, Scots law (and that of the UK as a whole) has been increasingly overrun in a number of policy areas by the relentless march of EC law, including, for example, in the commercial, financial markets and employment spheres. EC law is likely to remain a major influence on the development of Scots law in the years to come.

The revival of Scots law: the Scottish Parliament

In contrast to the demise of distinct Scottish principles since the Act of Union in 1707, over recent years there has been a re-emergence of distinct and separate Scottish legal rules in a number of policy areas. This has occurred as a result of the advent of the new Scottish Parliament at Holyrood in Edinburgh. The new Parliament was created after the "Campaign for a Scottish Assembly" was launched in 1988 with the aim of setting up a new legislative body in Scotland and a transference of power back from London. It is perhaps somewhat paradoxical, then, that the Scottish Parliament itself was created by a piece of Westminster legislation – the Scotland Act 1998. The Act was passed following a referendum, wherein the Scottish people voted in favour of the new devolved body. Since its inception, the Parliament has been empowered to legislate for its people in a number of "devolved" policy areas. The extent to which this amounts to any real "revival" of Scots law is debatable and the Scottish Parliament has at best received a mixed reception thus far. Nevertheless, the inception of the Scottish Parliament has certainly led to increased legislation in Scotland and a parting of ways with English approaches in a number of policy areas, such as freedom of information, sexual educational policy within schools and anti-smoking legislation. The composition, work and legislation of the Scottish Parliament as a source of Scots law are considered in Chapter 2.

Essential Facts

- Scots law is a mixed legal system, which means it has been influenced by both classic legal schools: the Common law system, derived from England; and the Civil law system, derived from Roman law.
- The Scottish legal system has a rich heritage and has been influenced by a number of historical factors including feudal law (from England), Canon law (of the Roman Catholic Church), Roman law, English law and European Community Law.
- The key early influences were feudalism (a system of landownership) and other governance tools borrowed from England, beginning in the 11th century; Roman law, stemming from the foreign travel of law students, beginning in the 16th century and the works of institutional writers which were penned in the 17th, 18th and 19th centuries.
- The key modern influences are English law, which stemmed largely from legislation passed in the aftermath of the Act of Union in 1707 and the influence of the Judicial Committee of the House of Lords; and European Community law, which has become increasingly important since the UK joined in 1973.

2 SOURCES OF SCOTS LAW

The term "source" of law can hold different meanings. As noted in Chapter 1, Scots law has evolved over the best part of a thousand years, being influenced by unsophisticated customary rules, Canon (or church) law, Roman law, Feudal law and English law. The notion of a source of law may also relate to the rationale behind the inception of a particular legal rule. In this sense, religious doctrines, social trends, political expediency and economic efficiency may underlie the adoption of particular legal principles. Although these historical and philosophical influences account for the origins of Scots law, they do not answer the question as to why particular rules are binding upon us. If a rule is to be binding then it must be derived from one or more recognised sources of law, known as formal sources.

FORMAL SOURCES

The formal sources include:

- legislation; and
- common law:

Common law sources encompass:

- judicial precedent;
- institutional writings;
- custom; and
- equity.

Legislation

Legislation may be considered the primary source of law and is typically the result of the expression of will of a rule-making body which exhibits some form of state legitimacy or authority. The volume of legislation affecting Scotland has increased considerably over recent years. Modern society is complex and, reflecting this, Parliament has deemed it necessary to legislate in the name of regulating and facilitating multifarious activities in society. Beginning at the time of the Industrial Revolution in the 1850s, successive governments found it necessary to propose laws in areas such as employment, housing, health and social services, education and the environment. Current trends show no sign of the legislative juggernaut abating, leading some to claim that now we live in a "nanny-State", where Parliament has become increasingly guilty of over-regulating our lives.

Over recent years there has also been an increase in the number of bodies empowered to legislate for the people of Scotland. This power to legislate arises either constitutionally or, increasingly, by empowering legislation (known as "delegated legislation"). Those bodies empowered to enact laws applicable to Scotland include the UK Parliament, the Scottish Parliament, the European Union and various individuals and organisations delegated the right to do so.

UK legislation

Constitutional issues. As noted, the (now) UK Parliament in Westminster was first established in 1707. The Parliament is bicameral in nature, which means that it comprises two legislative houses – the elected House of Commons and the non-elected House of Lords. Parliament (or the Legislature) should be distinguished from the Government (the Executive). In short, the role of the Executive, which is headed by the Prime Minister and ministerial Cabinet, is to propose new legislation, while Parliament's role is to enact it. Unlike other jurisdictions, there is no strict separation of powers in the law-making process in the UK; the Executive overlaps with and is part of the Legislature (and as we shall see below, the judiciary also currently overlaps with both the Executive and the Legislature). Given the control that the Executive is normally able to exert over Parliament, the legislative function is in practice often dominated by the Executive.

Legislation enacted by the UK Parliament is known as a "statute". With the monarch's political role now reduced in practical terms to a cosmetic one, UK legislation represents the will of the highest law-making power in the UK. This notion stems from the fact that, in constitutional terms, the UK can be characterised as a "parliamentary democracy". This means that, except in particular spheres where it has voluntarily conceded power (for example, on matters now governed by the European Union and those devolved to the new Scottish Parliament), the UK Parliament, as the supreme legislative body in the UK, is in theoretical terms empowered to enact any legal provisions whatsoever. While in the interests of political expediency Parliament may in practice try to refrain from enacting unpopular legislation, unlike legislative bodies in other countries (such as Canada, the USA and France), the UK Parliament is not required to act in accordance with some higher authority such as a written constitution. Thus, primary legislation of the UK Parliament cannot be challenged in, nor overturned by, the courts of the land (although the Human Rights Act 1998, discussed below, provides a challenge to law-makers in this sense).

Scottish Acts. After the Act of Union of 1707 established the new Westminster Parliament, Scotland was generally entitled to retain its own distinct laws and legal system (subject to the proviso that these could be overturned and amended by Acts of the Westminster Parliament). The old Scottish Parliament was politically a largely primitive (and undemocratic) affair with little long-lasting influence. Most Acts of the old Scottish Parliament have been repealed by subsequent UK legislation or, because of changing social norms and their lack of modern relevance, have fallen into desuetude (disuse) and are no longer considered enforceable.

Since the Union of the Parliaments, all UK legislation has applied to Scotland unless the contrary is expressly stated. Owing to pressures on parliamentary time and, perhaps, lack of interest, it has been common for UK-wide Acts of Parliament to include additional, bolted-on sections, which apply only to Scotland, with a view to preserving the different legal doctrines and rules that exist north of the Border. Heavy criticism has been levelled against this practice (colloquially known as "putting a kilt" on the Act) because it has failed to preserve the uniqueness of Scots law by largely ignoring its nuances and importing, wholesale, English legal principles. A contrary argument might be that, in the interests of efficiency and certainty, there is much to be said for harmonising particular spheres of law (such as that relating to commercial matters) across the whole of the UK. Readers may come to their own conclusions as they encounter examples of this practice in different areas. A pertinent example is the (original) Sale of Goods Act 1893, which imported a number of English common law principles into Scots law.

Finally, certain UK Parliament Acts apply *only* to Scotland. This is denoted by the word "Scotland" appearing in brackets towards the end of the title of the Act − for example, the Bankruptcy (Scotland) Act 1985. The scope for Scotland-only Acts of the UK Parliament has been greatly reduced by the advent of the new Scottish Parliament (discussed below) which has been given the devolved right to legislate for Scotland in a number of areas.

Types of Acts. There are a number of different Acts of the UK Parliament, including General Acts, Local Acts and Personal Acts. General Acts are the most important as these apply to the whole community. Local Acts, as the name suggests, are those which are restricted to a particular locality. These are not very common as most local legislative provisions are enacted by local authorities through the issuance of byelaws (see below). An example of a

Local Act is the Ipswich Market Act 2004 which regulated traffic use when there were local markets taking place. Personal Acts are relevant only to a particular person or group of persons. Many early Personal Acts pertained to the powers of the monarchy. There have been no Personal Acts since 1987.

An Act's antecedent is known as a "Bill". All General Acts begin as Public Bills. The bulk of Public Bills are brought to Parliament by government in its role as Executive. Hence, such Bills are generally promoted by the Government Minister responsible for the particular policy area (or "portfolio") to which the proposed legislation relates. Some Public Bills, however, are brought forward by Members of Parliament (MPs) who are not members of government. These MPs are granted the opportunity to bring forward their own proposals by means of a parliamentary ballot. These proposals are known as Private Members' Bills. Given the fact that government has a tight timetable within which to enact its wide-ranging, intended statutory provisions, very few of these Bills become Acts. The tight timescales for their enactment mean that they are very easily "talked out" by opponents and, in practice, Private Members' Bills normally require government support to succeed.

Local and Personal Acts are brought as Private Bills. The reader should not confuse Private Bills with Private Members' Bills (which, as noted above, are in fact Public Bills). A Private Bill seeks the enactment of a piece of legislation that gives powers or benefits to a particular group of persons, such as a local council or private corporation. Such Bills are brought by the party seeking the requisite powers, petitioning Parliament in a process which is similar to court hearings. The Bills are normally referred to a panel of MPs where those seeking the powers may put forward their case and those who may be adversely affected by the provision may lodge complaints. Bills which exhibit features of both Public and Private Bills – ie those primarily of relevance to a particular group of persons but which may impact upon the public in general – are termed "hybrid" Bills. They are subject to Parliamentary procedures that relate to both Public and Private Bills. The most recent example of a hybrid Bill was the Crossrail Act 2008 which received Royal Assent on 22 July 2008.

The rationale behind Acts of Parliament. Generally speaking, the fundamental purpose of all Acts of Parliament is to act on some policy initiative and bring about new law. Some Acts, however, do have particular technical purposes that denote a particular classification. Codifying Acts, for example, can be considered as "tidy up" exercises, designed to assimilate all existing law – both common law and perhaps other statutes – in a given area and frame it within a single piece of legislation. An oft-cited example is the original Sale of Goods Act 1893, which brought together the common law and statutory provisions that had hitherto existed.

In a similar vein, sometimes the purpose of legislation is to bring together existing Acts of Parliament that presently govern an area of law. Generally, the purpose of these provisions is to render the law clearer and more accessible. Such legal enactments are termed consolidation Acts. A pertinent example is the Health and Safety at Work etc Act 1974, which drew together the strands of a number of other provisions (including the Factories Act 1961 and the Offices, Shops and Railway Premises Act 1963) in one place.

A declaratory Act is one which seeks to restate the law. Government might deem this necessary, particularly in the aftermath of a controversial, unpopular or inconvenient court decision. One striking example is the War Damage Act 1965, which was enacted in the aftermath of a House of Lords' decision (sitting as a court) which compelled the Government to pay out hefty compensation for its destruction of British-owned oil fields at the time of the Korean War (*Burmah Oil Co (Burma Trading) Ltd* v *Lord Advocate* (1964)). This Act, incidentally, is a rare example of the enactment of what can be termed as "retrospective" legislation by the state, which, in this instance, nullified the hitherto valid claims of other oil-field owners for compensation. Legislating in a retrospective fashion may at times entail human rights concerns (see the discussion on human rights below).

Statute Law Revision Acts are designed to repeal existing legislation which has become obsolete or is no longer of relevance in modern society. A Law Reform (Miscellaneous Provisions) Act is a common, but arguably unsatisfactory, method by which minor amendments can be made to various areas of law at the same time. The lack of focus of such Acts may lead to poor legislating. A recent example is the Law Reform (Miscellaneous Provisions) (Scotland) Act 1990, which governed such diverse areas as charity law, the provision of legal services, licensing, evidence by children at criminal trials, treatment of offenders, drug trafficking confiscation orders, arbitration and homelessness.

Legislative provisions with the particular aim of amending or updating a previous piece of legislation are known as amendment Acts. For instance, the Race Relations (Amendment) Act 2000 brought about particular reforms of the Race Relations Act 1976. If any ambiguity exists between the provisions of the original legislation and those of the amendment Act, the provisions of the latter will be enforced as they represent the latest expression of the will of Parliament.

The legislative process for Public Bills. Here we focus on the law-making process for Public Bills – being the most important kind of legislation passed by the Westminster Parliament. Acts of the Parliament are subject to a somewhat convoluted, and often lengthy, legislative process.

Procedure outwith Parliament. Before examining the parliamentary law-making procedure, it is important to note that pre-parliamentary processes have a major impact on the composition of any new Bill. The life of any Public Bill (except for Private Members' Bills) begins with the Government considering what policy measures it wishes to put to Parliament. At this early stage, government may be influenced by a number of factors and advice may be obtained and consultation sought from a number of internal and external bodies. In particular, advice may be sought, and representation obtained, from government departmental and inter-departmental committees. With regard to particularly technical areas of law (oft-termed "lawyers' law") – for example, company, partnership and insolvency law – law reform bodies such as the Law Commission of England and Wales and the Scottish Law Commission may also be called upon for input. Independent pressure and interest groups may also seek to influence the policy-making process. Over recent years, these cultural and occupational groupings have gained importance as players in the political game. They campaign in a number of policy areas including animal welfare, education, the environment, equality for ethnic minorities, health, housing, rural affairs and welfare rights. Some groups have more political clout than others and, similarly, their methods of gaining influence on policy vary widely from petitioning government and writing to MPs, to urban terrorism and violent protests.

Consultation also takes place in the public eye. Governments may publish Green Papers setting out broad policy ideas and inviting representations thereon from the public. Similarly, White Papers, which entail more defined expressions of legislative intent, may also be published. It should be noted, though, that the Government is not required to issue either Green or White papers prior to publishing a Bill. Public consultation does not normally allow the public to vote on any proposed provision. In respect of measures of particular legislative importance, however, a public referendum may be called. A referendum was held in respect of the establishment of the new Scottish Parliament.

When the consultation period has ended, a Bill will be presented to Parliament. The drafting of the Bill is undertaken by "Parliamentary Counsel" (special legal draftsmen) on the advice of the government department concerned. The drafting process can be long and arduous. Poor drafting may lead to problems with the interpretation of statutes (discussed below) and may provide loopholes in the law for lawyers to exploit. In the name of

open government, and perhaps to alleviate difficulties with interpretation, in
1997 the new Labour Government announced its intention to publish an
increased number of "draft Bills".

Stages of the parliamentary process. A Bill may be introduced
in either of the two parliamentary chambers: the House of Commons
or the House of Lords. Given that the bulk of legislation arises from the
Executive (government), most Acts originate in the House of Commons.
Indeed, certain provisions, eg those relating to taxation and finance, must be
introduced in the House of Commons.

The House of Commons, historically the lower-status House but now
at the heart of the legislative process, comprises 646 MPs, including 59
Scottish MPs. The MPs are elected on a constituency, "first past the post",
basis for a period of up to 5 years. It should also be noted that, at the time of
writing, the House of Lords is undergoing what has become a very drawn-
out process of reform and its future make-up and legislative powers are
unknown. At this juncture the House of Lords comprises four different sorts
of members or "peers", namely: 600 or so "life peers" – life-long members
appointed by the Crown (in practice, appointed on the advice of the Prime
Minister although the process for appointment has become more transparent
of late); up to 12 Law Lords; a small number of Anglican Archbishops and
senior diocesan bishops of the Church of England; and 92 hereditary peers
who hold a historic birthright to sit in the house (this residual number is
what remains of the 700 hereditary peers that hitherto dominated the House
of Lords). The majority of hereditary peerages were recently abolished by
way of the House of Lords Act 1999 and the remainder look set to follow
when the ongoing reforms to the House of Lords are completed. In this
writer's view, while not underestimating the service of particular hereditary
peers to the House over the years, it is certainly an untenable proposition
that in a modern, democratic society the privileged few should assume a role
in the law-making process of the land simply because of the family name
they bear.

The reform of the House of Lords has been fraught with difficulty,
however. After a spate of "false-starts" the timetable for reform has still to
be finalised. While there seems to be a general appetite for retention of some
form of second chamber within Parliament to act as a brake and monitor on
the otherwise oft-untrammelled power of government, any clear view on
the future constitution and powers of the House of Lords remains elusive.
Various options for reform – which have all been previously rejected by
Parliament – include a fully appointed House, a fully elected House and
various combinations of the two. For a recent update on the state of reform

of the House of Lords, refer to http://www.parliament.uk/documents/upload/HLLReformChronology.pdf.

Procedure in Parliament

- *First reading*: The Bill is normally presented at first reading. This is a formal exercise where MPs are informed about the proposed legislation and a date is announced for the second reading of the Bill.

- *Second reading*: The first parliamentary debate on the Bill, a discussion of the Bill's main policy themes will take place with Government Ministers and their Opposition "shadow" equivalents both making opening and closing speeches. A vote will take place as to whether the Bill should proceed or not.

- *Committee stage*: The Bill is examined by a parliamentary committee comprising MPs reflecting the balance of political power in the House in which the Bill originated. The Committee then analyses the detail of the Bill in a comprehensive scrutinising process.

- *Report stage*: Upon completion of its analysis the Committee reports back to the House, often with a number of proposed amendments. These amendments may be discussed and voted on in the House. Moreover, new amendments may be lodged at this time.

- *Third reading*: This may take place immediately after the report stage. The Bill is read a final time, which in effect amounts to a motion that it be passed.

If the Bill completes its journey in the Commons, it will then be considered in much the same way by the House of Lords. It should be noted that presently the Lords can only, in general, delay an Act for a year. By using the Parliament Act 1949, the House of Commons can ultimately force through any legislation without the consent of the Lords. Such a move is considered politically controversial, however, and has occurred on only four occasions since the 1949 Act was passed – the most recent being the controversial Hunting Act in 2004, which banned the hunting of foxes with dogs. At the end of the parliamentary process, the Bill must be forwarded to the monarch for Royal Assent before it can become law. By constitutional convention (a customary rule of the constitution), however, the monarch would never refuse to give such consent. If the monarch disapproves of any proposed Act, he or she may comment on this in private only. In what may be an apocryphal tale, when Parliament in the late 19th century sought to make male homosexuality and lesbianism a crime, Queen Victoria viewed that the criminalisation of the latter was inappropriate on the basis that she did not believe that the practice existed!

An Act which has become law will often come into force (or "commence") whenever Royal Assent is given. However, in order to allow affected parties to make preparation for any new law, as is often the case, an Act will commence at a later date – either with reference to a time-frame expounded in the Act itself or where the provision empowers a Government Minister or some other person to set a date for commencement.

Legislation of the Scottish Parliament

At the time of writing, the Scottish Parliament is in its third parliamentary session. In its second session, between 2003 and 2007, the Parliament enacted some 66 Acts. Ten Acts have already been passed in the current session, including some important legislation such as the Judiciary and Courts (Scotland) Act 2008 and the Graduate Endowment Abolition (Scotland) Act 2008. Unlike the UK Parliament, the Scottish Parliament is unicameral – ie there is only one legislative chamber. The Parliament comprises 129 Members of the Scottish Parliament (MSPs). Of this cohort, 73 are elected on a "first past the post", constituency basis and a further 56 are appointed on regional lists via a proportional representation procedure known as the "additional member system". The Executive in the new Scottish devolved law-making arrangement (the Scottish Government, currently a minority SNP administration) is composed of a First Minister and a number of Ministers, who are also MSPs. Hence, again, as is the case at Westminster, there is no strict separation of powers between the executive and legislative functions.

The Scottish Parliament's legislative powers are "devolved", ie they have arisen from powers handed down by the Westminster Parliament via the Scotland Act 1998. This fact is important in that the Scottish Parliament's powers can therefore generally be considered as subordinate to the authority of the UK Parliament which arises constitutionally.

The Scotland Act empowers the new Parliament to enact law in all policy matters pertaining to Scotland save particular "reserved" areas which remain the exclusive preserve of the UK Parliament. These reserved matters include: UK constitutional issues; foreign affairs; defence; fiscal and economic policy (although the Scottish Parliament has limited, albeit, as of yet unused, tax-raising powers); social security; and employment. Under s 29(1) of the Scotland Act, the Scottish Parliament cannot encroach upon any reserved matter.

Despite the wide range of reserved matters, the policy areas that remain do, however, represent a significant opportunity for the Parliament to

enact legislation. It should be noted, however, that, given the constitutional supremacy of the UK Parliament, even in respect of devolved areas, the UK Parliament could continue to legislate for Scotland (and this is expressly provided for in s 28(7) of the Scotland Act). It would be somewhat unsatisfactory, however, if, after setting up the new Scottish body, the Westminster Parliament continually rode roughshod over the devolved powers when it deemed fit to do so. In what can be considered a very British solution (because an agreement is made by a non-legal convention rather than strict legal means) such issues are covered by the Sewell Convention (named after Lord Sewell), by virtue of which the Westminster Parliament would encroach in devolved areas only with the Scottish Parliament's consent,
Ｘ through what are termed "Sewell motions". Sewell motions themselves have become an issue of controversy, however. It was originally intended that Sewell motions would be used only on rare occasions where it was deemed more convenient for Westminster to legislate in a given area across the UK as a whole. At the time of writing there have been some 86 Sewell motions since 1999 and the previous Scottish Executive was subject to the criticism that it has used these cross-border agreements to shunt politically difficult decisions south. A recent example of legislation passed via a Sewell motion that exemplifies such controversies is the Civil Partnership Act 2004.

The legislative process. The law-making processes of the Scottish Parliament differ somewhat from those of its UK counterpart. The Scotland Act itself makes scant provision concerning legislative procedures, save that by virtue of s 22 the Parliament must adopt Standing Orders to ensure that any Bill proposed is subject to three readings prior to adoption (Standing Orders of the Scottish Parliament, Edition 2 (20 January 2000)). While a summary is provided below, for a detailed review of the Parliamentary Procedures, refer to http://www.scottish.parliament.uk/ business/parliamentaryprocedure/index.htm.

Care must be taken to ensure that the Scottish Parliament passes only those laws it is competent to pass. In this sense, a number of safeguards are built into the law-making procedures. First, when a Bill is brought to Parliament it must be accompanied by a written statement from the Presiding Officer outlining his or her view on whether the proposed Act falls within the scope of the devolved powers. (The Presiding Officer is an MSP, but is politically impartial. The role of the Presiding Officer is, generally, to chair parliamentary meetings and ensure that the legislative process runs in an appropriate and lawful manner.)

Akin to the legislative process at Westminster, most Bills are the product of executive action. Bills may on occasion be brought by individual MSPs (termed "Members' Bills"). Where the Bill is brought by the Scottish Executive (known as an "Executive Bill"), it must also be accompanied by a written statement from the appropriate Minister affirming that the legislative proposals fall within the scope of the Parliament's competence. In addition, the Bill should be accompanied by: a policy memorandum outlining the policy objectives of the legislation; a statement of any consultation which has preceded the Bill; explanatory notes, summarising the Bill's contents; a statement of consideration of alternative policy approaches; and assessment of the Bill's impact on a variety of factors including equal opportunities, human rights, sustainable development and island communities.

The parliamentary process. The parliamentary process for Bills varies according to the type of Bill being proposed. The following represents the most common procedure:

- *Stage 1*: The Bill is first forwarded to a committee dealing with the relevant area of policy to which the Bill relates (known as the "lead committee"). The committee considers the general principles of the Bill and reports back to Parliament. The general scope and provisions of the Bill are then considered by Parliament in the light of the committee's report. It is possible at this stage for the Bill to be referred back to the lead committee for a further report on any aspect of the Bill before the Parliament makes its decision.

- *Stage 2*: If Parliament has agreed upon the general principles of the Bill, it is then sent back to the lead committee or alternatively to a committee of the whole Parliament (or in some cases both), where the Bill's provisions are scrutinised and amendments can be proposed.

- *Stage 3*: The amended Bill is then considered by Parliament as a whole and a vote is taken to decide whether the Bill will be passed or not. Additional amendments may be lodged at this point.

If the Bill is passed by the Parliament, the Presiding Officer is duty bound to forward it to the monarch for Royal Assent. Prior to this occurring, however, and within 4 weeks of the passing of the Bill, by virtue of s 33 of the Scotland Act 1998, a number of personnel (namely the Advocate General, the Attorney-General or the Lord Advocate) can refer the Bill to the Judicial Committee of the Privy Council to examine whether it falls within the legislative scope of the Parliament. (Scotland's legal personnel are discussed in more detail in Chapter 5. The Privy Council is discussed in Chapter 3.)

The Constitutional Reform Act 2005, creating a Supreme Court in the UK commencing operation from October 2009 will abolish the appellate jurisdiction of the House of Lords (sitting as a court). Under the new arrangements the Privy Council functions will also become subsumed within the new Supreme Court.

As a further monitor on the Scottish Parliament's legislative powers, under s 35 of the Scotland Act 1998, the Secretary of State for Scotland (a member of government at Westminster) may issue an order forbidding the Presiding Officer from forwarding the Bill for Royal Assent. The general prohibitions on law-making for the Scottish Parliament are set out in s 29 and include provision that the Scottish Parliament may not legislate in respect of reserved matters, make laws contrary to European Community law or the European Convention on Human Rights and Fundamental Freedoms, legislate for another country or territory or legislate contrary to certain specified Westminster statutes including the Human Rights Act 1998, the Scotland Act 1998 and the Act of Union 1707.

Delegated legislation of the UK Parliament

As noted above, in modern times we have experienced a perceived, rising need for the enactment of more and more legislation in a multitude of different policy areas. The lengthy and complex UK legislative process has already been alluded to and, given time constraints alone, it is not possible to enact primary legislation to meet all perceived policy need. Statutory provisions, therefore, do not always originate directly from primary legislation but rather enter into force by way of what can be termed as "delegated legislation" (or secondary legislation). In short, delegated legislation encompasses situations in which the right to legislate has been delegated by Parliament to some other person or entity. There are two main types of delegated legislation: statutory instruments (or regulations) and byelaws.

Statutory instruments. Under powers bestowed by an enabling (or parent) Act of Parliament (a pertinent example is the Health and Safety at Work etc Act 1974), Government Ministers may be vested with the right to formulate their own statutory instruments within the ambit of the Act. Ministers are also given latitude by primary and secondary legislation to take policy decisions within their ministerial portfolio. For example, the Home Secretary is empowered to take decisions pertaining to individual immigration and citizenship cases. The Act of Parliament empowering Ministers to enact delegated legislation may itself prescribe merely a general policy framework which requires to be implemented in practice by the Minister concerned through delegated legislation and policy decisions. Under the Statutory

Instruments Act 1946, these ministerial legislative measures are termed "statutory instruments".

Government Ministers may also issue "Orders in Council" made in pursuance of what can be termed the "Royal Prerogative". The Royal Prerogative relates to a number of residual powers of the monarch which the Government is now able to implement by virtue of its modern constitutional status as "the Queen in Parliament". Such Orders are enacted when the Queen's representatives in the Privy Council effectively rubber-stamp draft Orders presented to them by government. Unfettered prerogative powers are an oddity in modern society and their continued existence in modern times can be considered as an affront to democracy. Nevertheless, some important powers are vested in government through the Royal Prerogative, including the right to declare war and the right to enter into treaties with other nations. In other cases, the right to make Orders in Council in specified situations does not arise constitutionally but has been expressly conferred upon the Crown (and hence government) through Acts of Parliament. For example, the Emergency Powers (Defence) Act 1939 empowered the Crown (and, in practice, therefore the Government) to make Orders in Council to ensure public safety after an outbreak of war.

Byelaws. Much law enacted is of a local nature, affecting only particular local communities. In this sense, local authorities are empowered to enact "byelaws" which apply to their geographical areas of governance, primarily by the Local Government (Scotland) Act 1973 (as amended). The enactment of byelaws allows the local authority to undertake a number of regulatory functions and tackle local nuisances and associated community problems. Byelaws may be passed in a number of different areas including the regulation of alcohol consumption, the licensing of betting shops, saunas and tattoo parlours, and prohibiting ball games in public places and fishing in certain rivers. Byelaws do not normally come into force until they are confirmed by some governmental authority (generally a Government Minister).

Delegated legislation created by the Scottish courts. It may seem unconstitutional for courts to be granted the power to enact laws. Yet particular Acts of Parliament vest in the Scottish courts the power to prescribe new rules for court procedure. An "Act of Sederunt" is a rule formulated by the Court of Session under delegated powers (primarily under the Administration of Justice (Scotland) Act 1933, s 16) by which it may alter its own procedure or that in the sheriff courts. Other primary Acts of Parliament, including the Sheriff Courts (Scotland) Act 1971, also allow the Court of

Session to enact Acts of Sederunt. In a similar fashion, under the Criminal Procedure (Scotland) Act 1975, the High Court of Justiciary may also pass "Acts of Adjournal" to bring about reform of criminal court procedure.

Sub-delegated legislation. Sub-delegated legislation, whereby the party empowered to enact delegation by Parliament passes the right on to another, is relatively rare. Most parent Acts of Parliament allow for one level of delegation only; indeed, there is a presumption that Parliament intended sub-delegation not to take place. This presumption has its origins in a well-established, common law rule of agency that an agent (or delegate) cannot delegate. However, sub-delegation does take place from time to time. An oft-cited example of this arose under the Emergency Powers (Defence) Act 1939, enacted at the time of the Second World War. The Act enabled Ministers to make orders which provided authority for others to make particular directions which, in turn, allowed others to issue certain licences in specified circumstances.

Delegated legislation: checks and balances. There are a number of ways in which the exercise of delegated legislation can be monitored in practice. The principal control stems from the enabling Act of Parliament itself, which will set out the legislative framework or area of discretion within which the delegated legislation can be crafted.

Monitoring may also take place within and outwith Parliament. Internal monitoring within Parliament may also be carried out, primarily under ss 4–7 of the Statutory Instruments Act 1946. In this sense, ministerial statutory instruments must be "laid" before either House of Parliament. MPs are then able to scrutinise the instrument for a 3-week period prior to it coming into force. While this in itself does not provide any real check on ministerial discretion, one of two further parliamentary monitoring procedures will normally apply, known as the "negative" or "affirmative" resolution procedure. The negative resolution procedure will normally apply, in which event a parliamentary vote may strike down the instrument. Where the affirmative procedure applies, the instrument will not come into force until it is approved by a vote in Parliament. It has been argued that, in light of government's dominant role in Parliament, instruments are rarely nullified in these ways in practice.

More direct control is exercised over delegated legislation when statutory instruments are scrutinised by a Joint Committee on Statutory Instruments, comprising members from both chambers in Parliament. The committee can refer the delegated legislation back to either House on any of eight specified grounds as well as a "catch-all" discretionary basis.

On the basis of a petition brought by an affected party with "standing" to bring such an action, the Court of Session may overturn any exercise of delegated legislation under a process termed "judicial review". If it appears that a particular statutory instrument is beyond the powers of its enabling Act (*ultra vires*), which may include circumstances in which it is subject to some procedural irregularity, has been enacted by the wrong person or body, is manifestly unreasonable or motivated by improper considerations, then the Court of Session may strike the instrument down. It should be noted that courts are not in general concerned with the merits of the legislation, but rather whether or not its enactment was legal under various grounds, including those referred to above. It is also important to reiterate that, given the doctrine of UK parliamentary supremacy, courts are not empowered to strike down a primary Act of Parliament; but the judiciary may, however, cast aside the exercise of delegated legislation – which in itself is not an expression of the will of Parliament.

Delegated legislation of the Scottish Parliament

In one sense, all Acts of the Scottish Parliament amount to delegated legislation in that the Scottish Parliament's powers to enact legislation are devolved from the Scotland Act 1998 – a piece of Westminster legislation. As noted in Chapter 1, prior to a Bill receiving Royal Assent there is a cooling-off period during which it may be subject to review by the Judicial Committee of the Privy Council (or, in the future, the Supreme Court) to ensure that it falls within the ambit of the Parliament's powers. However, given that legislation of the Scottish Parliament is not constitutionally supreme, it can be subject to judicial review even after it has been given Royal Assent. To some extent this gives courts a new, constitutional role: for the first time courts are able to take issue with Acts of Parliament, albeit those of the devolved Scottish Parliament. None of the above, however, detracts from the general principle of Westminster Parliamentary supremacy.

A recent example of a challenge to legislation of the Scottish Parliament can be found in the high-profile case of Noel Ruddle. Noel Ruddle was a psychopath who had been sent to be detained indefinitely in a secure mental institution in 1991 after he had killed his neighbour with a Kalashnikov rifle. However, as a result of a loophole in mental health legislation, and amidst a howl of protests, he was released in 1999. A number of other individuals concurrently incarcerated in secure mental institutions and in a similar position to Ruddle subsequently sought their release too. In response, the Scottish Executive closed this *lacuna* in the law with the enactment of the Mental Health (Scotland) Act 1999. Normally this move would amount to locking the stable door after the horse had bolted but the law was also altered retrospectively and hence nullified the rights of action of the parties now seeking release. This Act was challenged in the Court of Session, on the basis that the retrospective nature of the legislation, which defeated what might otherwise be a valid claim in law, was contrary to the Parliament's human rights obligations. We should perhaps be thankful that the claim was not successful, though; the new Act stood and Ruddle's successors remained incarcerated (see *A* v *Scottish Ministers* (2001)).

The Scottish Parliament, like Westminster, may delegate powers to Ministers and others. Again, any ministerial instruments must be "laid" before Parliament. The instruments are then referred to a committee within whose remit the legislation falls (the "lead committee") or a special subordinate legislation committee. The committee's role, in general, is to ensure that the instrument is not *ultra vires* or outwith the powers set out in the enabling Act, it is properly drafted, and it does not encroach upon any reserved matter. Any adverse reports can then be debated in the Scottish Parliament.

In a similar vein to Westminster, instruments are subject to one of two parliamentary procedural checks. Many instruments will become law at the end of a 40-day period unless a motion is passed in Parliament that the delegated legislation be struck out. Rarely, instruments will not come into effect until they are afforded express approval in Parliament. Like primary Acts of the Scottish Parliament, delegated legislation is also, of course, reviewable in the Court of Session. Scottish parliamentary procedures regarding delegated legislation are available to view at http://www.scottish. parliament.uk/business/so/sto-4.ht

Delegated legislation: advantages and disadvantages

Delegated legislation is clearly a necessity in any modern legal system. Its principal advantage is that it provides a solution to the vast parliamentary time and resources which would be required in any attempt to pass all required regulation by way of primary legislation; in contrast, delegated legislation can be enacted quickly. This may be important in meeting the requirements of novel contingencies, regulating new, hitherto unanticipated technologies and reacting to shifting social mores. Delegated legislation is key in emergency situations where swift action is axiomatic, such as during wartime. Finally, in particularly technical areas of policy, detailed legislation and policy decisions can be crafted by specialists in the particular field rather than by a largely ignorant Parliament.

While delegated legislation is necessary, it may, however, be a "necessary evil" in that it is democratically deficient – parties other than elected MPs are empowered to take decisions which affect the public. Such concerns are exacerbated by the limited control which is exercised over delegated legislation in practice. These claims may be particularly pertinent in respect of the oft-extensive legislative clout wielded by Government Ministers. Of course the UK Parliament does have some means of reining in the excesses of ministerial legislative power but, given the dearth of time and resources available to the monitoring committees, it has been seriously doubted whether they are practically of much effect.

The court process of judicial review is also somewhat unsatisfactory. The Court of Session is unable to intervene of its own volition and can only act when a party petitions it for judicial review. The often exorbitant costs involved in litigation of this sort, and the limited availability of legal aid, may militate against judicial review being sought through the courts. Even if an action is successful, a remedy is only granted after the wrong has taken place. Moreover, in many instances, the court may find itself constricted by the fact that, as noted above, judicial review does not provide the opportunity for a challenge on the merits of any given ministerial action; in short, statutory instruments may only be overturned on the basis that they are *ultra vires* of (ie outwith) the powers bestowed on the actor by the enabling Act. The modern trend is for such parent Acts to vest wide discretionary legislative powers in Ministers, which provides scant scope for challenge. Moreover, clauses in enabling Acts may empower a Minister to amend the terms of the Act itself through delegated legislation, which may effectively cut courts out of the loop. Such controversial provisions can be termed "Henry VIII clauses". However, the Human Rights Act 1998 has created a new battle ground in which ministerial actions can be challenged in the courtroom. (See, for example, *Pretty* v *United Kingdom* (2002); *R* v *A* (2001) (complainant's sexual history); *R* v *Lambert (Steven)* (2001); *Re S (Children)* (2002) (care order: implementation of care plan)). This impact of the Human Rights Act is discussed further below.

EC legislation

As noted in Chapter 1, law stemming from the European Union (EU) has become of increasing influence in the UK over recent years. As a result of increasing levels of social cohesion, UK citizens have since found themselves increasingly subject to EC legislative measures which have sought to harmonise a diverse range of tracts of law across the Member States.

Originally, of course, what is now the EU began life as the European Economic Community (EEC), established under the auspices of the Treaty of Rome in 1957. The EEC itself can be seen as a logical extension, into other trade areas, of the European Coal and Steel Community (ECSC) of 1951. The main purpose of the EEC was to bring about the harmonisation of its Member States' respective economic policies and the removal of international trade barriers. After initially regarding it with relative indifference, the UK finally became a member of the EEC in 1973.

The Treaty of Rome has been followed by other international agreements. The Single European Act of 1986 established the European Community (EC) for the purpose of creating a single European internal market. This treaty was followed by the Treaty on European Union of 1992 (the "Maastricht Treaty") which led to the establishment of the EU with the view of facilitating increased social and political cohesion. Two further treaties – the Treaty of Amsterdam in 1997 and the Treaty of Nice in 2001 – were subsequently passed, primarily to address certain criticisms of the Maastricht Treaty which was seen as too much of a political compromise.

The recent growth to 27 members created momentum to drive forward a Treaty for the establishment of a European Constitution. As a notable historic fact, this treaty was signed on 29 October 2004 in the same room as the early European pioneers put pen to paper on the EEC Treaty in 1957. The European Constitution, however, has been dogged by controversy. While some commentators have claimed that the Constitution represents no more than a "tidy-up exercise" for EU powers, others have suggested that it is a bridge too far which would herald the demise of national identity and the unwarranted inception of a new European super-state. In any case, for the Constitution Treaty to come into force all Member States must ratify it. In 2005, both France and the Netherlands rejected the Constitution, although Luxembourg voted in its favour. The UK introduced a Bill to approve the treaty via a referendum, but, perhaps to the relief of government, the failure of the Constitution's acceptance across Europe has stalled the domestic debate. The Constitution's replacement, the Treaty of Lisbon, was agreed upon by Member States in December 2007. Its terms were accepted without a referendum in the UK but rejection by Irish voters has again stalled its implementation.

The treaties referred to above can be considered as the primary legislation of the EU. The primary legislation has also given rise to a plethora of secondary legislation, which can be crafted in different ways. It is worth noting that, despite the inception of the EU, this secondary legislation is generally referred to as European Community or EC legislation. As one might imagine, in common with domestic secondary or delegated legislation, the secondary EC legislation must not conflict with the treaties. All EC law, in general, however, takes precedence over Member States' domestic law in a given area. If there is any ambiguity between a particular point of EC law and its Scottish equivalent, then the EC provision will take precedence (*R v Secretary of State for Transport, ex parte Factortame* (1990)).

Regulations. Regulations are binding upon all Member States and directly applicable without any need for enactment in the domestic law of the state concerned. This type of legislation must be published in the *Official Journal* of the EU and will normally come into effect on a date set out in the regulation itself. Regulations are also characterised by "direct effect". This means, for example, that Scottish citizens are able to enforce regulations directly through the domestic courts of the land. Additionally, given the supremacy of EC law, Member States are prohibited from enacting any domestic provisions which are contrary to the terms of the regulation. The decision as to what form an EC law provision will take is normally left to the Commission (see below).

Directives. Directives, unlike regulations, do not automatically enter the domestic law of Member States on their enactment. When a directive is passed, Member States will then be given a particular time frame within which to enact domestic legislation which is compatible with the aim of the directive. In this sense a directive may be brought into force, domestically speaking, either by the passing of an Act of Parliament or by delegated legislation. In the sphere of UK agency law, for example, the provisions of European Directive 86/653 were brought into force by the Commercial Agents (Council Directive) Regulations 1993 (a form of UK delegated legislation). Readers should not confuse EC regulations with UK domestic regulations (statutory instruments by Ministers or public bodies made under delegated powers).

The UK domestic courts have been encouraged by the House of Lords to take a progressive approach in interpreting domestic legislative measures which have sought to implement directives, in order to give effect to the meaning of the directive. In *Litster* v *Forth Dry Dock Co* (1989), for example, the House of Lords was willing to write into domestic provisions words not approved by Parliament in order to give effect to the provisions of the directive concerned.

In general, directives do not have direct effect. This means that parties are unable to enforce the provisions of a directive through the Scottish courts until the directive has been incorporated into domestic law. There have, however, been instances in which the European Court of Justice (ECJ) has held that a citizen of a Member State could enforce a directive directly against a public body which was an organ of the state. This kind of right will arise in circumstances where the time limit for implementation of the directive has passed, but it has not yet been incorporated into the Member State's domestic law, and the directive is sufficiently definite and precise, leaving little leeway for the state concerned in terms of enacting the provision. For case examples, see Case 148/78 *Pubblico Ministero* v *Ratti* (1979); *Marshall* v *Southampton and South-West Hampshire Area Health Authority* (1986). In the *Marshall* case a female employee, who was being forced to retire at the age of 62 (whereas the usual retirement age for men was 65), claimed that the health authority that employed her was acting in a discriminatory fashion contrary to (now) Article 141 of the EC Treaty and Equal Treatment Directive 76/207. The European Court of Justice held that, as the authority was a public body, it was bound to act within the terms of the directive, even though its terms had not been enacted into domestic law.

The result of the above approach can be considered somewhat inequitable, given that it would allow, for example, an employee in the public sector to enforce a directive in such circumstances against his or her employer but similar rights would not be available to an employee in the private sector. In view of this anomaly, the ECJ has also allowed directives to be directly enforced against private individuals and entities of Member States (this is known as "horizontal direct effect") in particular circumstances, although the case law to date can hardly be described as consistent. (See *von Colson* v *Land Nordrhein-Westfalen* (1984) and compare with *Marleasing SA* v *La Comercial Internacional de Alimentacion SA* (C-106/89) (1992). See, further, *Unilever Italia SpA* (C-443/98) (2000). In addition, the ECJ has held that a citizen may bring an action for damages for the failure of his or her Member State to bring its domestic law into line with a directive (*Francovich* v *Italian Republic* (1992); *Dillenkofer* v *Federal Republic of Germany* (C-178-9/94) (1996); *Porter* v *Attorney-General for Northern Ireland* (settled out of court on 26 June 1995)).

Decisions. Many hundreds of administrative decisions of the Commission or Council of Ministers are enacted annually. These decisions are addressed either to particular Member States or specified corporations or individuals. Decisions do not require to be enacted into domestic law and become directly binding on the addressee alone.

The EC law-making process. The EC law-making process is very unlike the UK's legislative procedures. EC legislation is crafted by way of a somewhat cumbersome interactive process among three of the EU's principal political organisations or "Institutions": the Commission; the Council of Ministers; and the European Parliament. The other two Institutions are the European Court of Justice (ECJ) and the Court of Auditors. The role of EU judicial bodies is discussed in Chapter 3.

The Institutions. The European Commission comprises some 27 commissioners (one for each Member State), each responsible for a particular area of EU activity. Commissioners are EU nationals and they act in an independent capacity from their Member States. This detachment of Commissioners from their respective homelands renders the Commission a pro-European body. The Commission has a number of functions, primarily its responsibility for proposing new legislative measures. It can also be considered as the guardian of the Treaties and, for example, it may raise an action against any Member State in the ECJ for an alleged failure to comply with Treaty provisions.

The Council of Ministers comprises ministerial representatives of the 27 Member States. Its composition may alter depending on the area of policy under discussion. In practice it is more concerned with safeguarding Member States' national interests than the overtly European Commission. The Council is the supreme law-making body in the EU and lies at the heart of the legislative procedures.

The European Parliament is the directly elected body of the EU. In this sense at least it is a democratic body, although it is not the principal law-making body in the EU in the same way that the UK Parliament is in respect of UK law. Some 785 members (known as Members of the European Parliament or MEPs) are elected by the 25 Member States in national elections on a constituency basis. MEPs do not sit in national groups in the Parliament but rather along political lines. The Parliament, which is unicameral in nature, is primarily an advisory mechanism but, as discussed below, this body does have a co-operative and consultative role to play in the legislative process which has, moreover, been strengthened over recent years.

Law-making processes. Given the complexity of the law-making process within the EU, the following discussion represents a mere snapshot. The Commission, as the Executive within the EU, is responsible for proposing new legislative measures. In short, when a proposed measure is drafted, it is sent to the Council of Ministers, and in turn forwarded to the Parliament. The Parliament may debate the measures and seek further representations from the Commission and then provide advice as to the appropriateness of the proposals to the Council of Ministers. At this stage the proposed legislation is scrutinised by a Council working group manned by civil servants drawn from all Member States. Ultimately, the decision to give the proposal binding force or not will generally lie with the Council.

Despite the traditionally subservient role of the Parliament in the law-making process, its legislative powers were substantially enhanced in the aftermath of the Single European Act 1986. This treaty introduced a new co-operation procedure which allows the Parliament either to accept or to take issue with the position (known as a "common position") taken by the Council. If the Parliament rejects the Council's position, this can only be ignored by the Council on the basis of unanimity. In the case of any Parliament amendment to the common position, a qualified majority of the Council may override such an amendment.

The Treaty on European Union 1992 gave the Parliament additional powers under the "co-decision" procedure. This vests in Parliament more substantial rights of consultation and, in practice, may afford the Parliament a right of veto over a Council decision and hence block legislation. The European Parliament's legislative power was increased again in the aftermath of the Treaty of Nice 2000, which was brought into effect on 1 February 2003. One might expect that if closer political and social integration between Member States becomes a reality, the influence of the democratically elected Parliament will increase further.

Statutory interpretation

The way in which statutes are interpreted has a major influence on the way in which legislation acts as a source of law. Statutory interpretation is therefore an important process by which, for example, a court must ascertain whether a particular piece of legislation applies to the facts at hand and, if so, what kind of effect that legislation has. If the issue is brought before a court, given that statutory interpretation is a question of law, it will always be determined by the judge and not the jury. Many disputes that reach the civil courts in fact boil down to a disagreement over statutory interpretation. In an ideal world statutes would be clear and precise, but even with the best of intentions (and draftsmen) this is not always the case. Throughout the years a number of rules have originated and been developed to assist courts in the interpretation of statutory terms that are confusing, nebulous or open to different interpretations. Given that words may hold different meanings, any form of verbal communication can be obscure at times. Legislation is no different.

The majority of statutory interpretation rules have been developed and refined by the courts themselves through the common law (for a discussion of common law sources, see below). A rare statutory intervention in this common law area is the Interpretation Act 1978. This Act provides scant assistance in most cases, however, and merely provides guidance of a general nature on the interpretation of words and phrases commonly used in legislation such as "land", "month" and "sheriff". The Act also allows certain assumptions to be drawn from wording in a piece of legislation unless the contrary is expressly stated in the statute concerned. So, for example, references in an Act to the masculine will be taken also to include the feminine, references to the singular will also include the plural and references to persons will encompass both natural persons and artificial legal entities (such as corporations).

Court rules of interpretation.
From a constitutional perspective, the role of the courts is to apply the desires of Parliament rather than deviate from statutes. As noted above, an Act may give rise to ambiguity, confusion and even, were the provision to be interpreted to the letter, absurdity. Against this backdrop, courts at times may take different approaches to interpreting statutes. Fundamentally, the two basic techniques that courts may choose between when interpreting legislative provisions are known as the "literal rule" and the "liberal rule". By virtue of the literal rule, the language in the Act is interpreted to the letter and not amplified in any sense by the court, even though this might lead to a somewhat illogical outcome that could not plausibly be said to have been the true intention of Parliament. A stark example of a literal interpretation can be seen in the unsatisfactory approach taken by the court in *Eddington v Robertson* (1895). At common law in the 19th century, a wife was entitled to a share of her husband's moveable estate (ie property that was not "heritable" such as land and buildings) if her husband died or divorced her. This general area of law was put onto a statutory footing by the Married Women's Property (Scotland) Act 1881, although, under the Act, this share in estate was available only when the husband died. Even though the absence of a right to share in the estate on divorce in the statute had almost certainly been caused by a draftsman's slip, the court refused to amend the wording to grant a divorced wife a remedy. It is likely that today the literal rule would be adopted only where the language in the statute concerned was plain and unambiguous.

The liberal rule, by contrast, allows the court to look at the general policy underpinning the Act, in addition to the wording of the Act itself, to ascertain what Parliament intended and to provide a more satisfactory result (as exemplified by the court in *Bonsor* v *Musicians' Union* (1956)). In this sense, the aims of Parliament may be gauged, for example, by the examination of various external and internal aids (see below).

Other techniques, such as the "mischief rule" and the "golden rule", may also be utilised in respect of statutory interpretation. However, these approaches are probably best viewed as mere variations on the two main (literal or liberal) rules. The mischief rule prescribes that the court interpret the provisions of an Act by reference to both the Act's express terms and the "mischief" (ie the evil or problem) that it was designed to alleviate (see

Corkery v *Carpenter* (1950)). The golden rule holds that courts must give effect to the intention of Parliament by according the terms of the Act their normal and common usage except where such an approach would cause an obvious absurdity or inconsistency. In such a case, the court could then interpret the provision in a liberal manner. A pertinent example is *Adler* v *George* (1964), in which the court held that the literal statutory wording which read "in the vicinity of" should be interpreted to include actions committed by the defendant in the case that took place within the area concerned, and not strictly speaking within its vicinity.

Internal aids. Help may sometimes be derived from within the Act itself. For example, most recent Acts contain their own interpretation section which defines the terms that are used in the Act. Courts may also have recourse to the notion of "interpretation in context", in which a court may consider the statute as a whole to interpret a particular part of it. Moreover, assistance may be found in parts of the Act itself including: the title, long or short; any preamble to the Act; Schedules to the Act; or any headings or subheadings.

External aids. External aids that courts may make reference to include the following: any reports that have preceded the Act (although it would appear that the only reports that can be referred to in this way are those which led up to the relevant Act, in order to discover the defects in the law that the new legislation sought to alleviate, such as Scottish Law Commission Reports – see, for example, *Keith* v *Texaco* (1977)); parliamentary debates on the provision concerned found in *Hansard* (the full and official reports of debates and other proceedings in Parliament) but such records can be referred only to where the legislation is ambiguous and the reference is to a statement made by a Minister which is sufficiently clear and precise – see *Pepper* v *Hart* (1993); other Acts on the same subject matter; the long-established, recognised use of the terms requiring interpretation; and views set out in esteemed textbooks.

Presumptions. As a final aid to interpretation, particular general pre-sumptions concerning the intention of Parliament can be made by the judge in the absence of any expressed intention to the contrary. These presumptions include: UK legislation is not intended to contravene international law; the legislation does not intend to usurp the jurisdiction of the courts; legislation should not have a retrospective effect (although some statutes will expressly provide for retroactivity, such as the War Damage Act 1965 and the War Crimes Act 1990); statutes that restrict liberty or impose taxes on the public are to be construed narrowly; it is presumed that the terms of statutes are not intended to be enforced against the Crown or its agents; and where the statute imposes criminal liability, unless the contrary is expressed, there is a presumption that *mens rea* (a guilty mind) is requisite for commission of the offence. It is also worth noting that in accordance with s 3 of the Human Rights Act 1998, all statutory provisions must be read in a way that is compatible with Convention rights.

Human rights and Scots law

Building from the above point, particular mention must be made of the impact of the European Convention on Human Rights (ECHR) and the Human Rights Act 1998 (HRA 1998) and of the way in which these legal provisions can be considered sources of Scots law. Although a mere Act of the UK Parliament, the effect of the HRA 1998 is to bestow itself with a somewhat special status as a source of law which provides a marked influence on Scots law in general. In short, the HRA 1998 partially incorporates the bulk of ECHR articles into domestic law in a number of ways, as shall be illustrated below. Prior to further discussion of the HRA 1998, it is useful to begin with a short précis of the ECHR itself.

The ECHR is an international treaty, established under the auspices of the Council of Europe in 1950, which sets out a number of fundamental freedoms and basic human rights in the form of "articles" and protocols (that have been added at later dates after the inception of the treaty, from time to time). These fundamental, basic entitlements – which can be termed "Convention rights" – are far-reaching and include:

- Article 2: the right to life
- Article 3: prohibition of torture
- Article 4: prohibition against slavery or forced labour
- Article 5: right to liberty and security
- Article 6: right to a fair trial
- Article 7: no punishment without law
- Article 8: right to respect for private and family life
- Article 9: freedom of thought, conscience and religion
- Article 10: freedom of expression
- Article 11: freedom of assembly and association
- Article 12: right to marry
- Article 13: right to an effective remedy
- Article 14: prohibition of discrimination

- Article 1, Protocol 1: protection of property
- Article 2, Protocol 1: right to education.

In the aftermath of the atrocities of the Second World War, a Council of Europe was formed with the intention of establishing some form of minimum code of human rights for the peoples of Europe. From this collaborative effort was born the ECHR. The UK became a signatory to the ECHR in 1950, although the treaty did not come into force until 1953. It is important to note that, as the ECHR is an international treaty, it did not follow from its ratification that its terms would become part of UK domestic law. Thus, the ECHR is not in itself a formal source of Scots law (see *Kaur* v *Lord Advocate* (1980); *Moore* v *Secretary of State for Scotland* (1985)). The ECHR has a partial force, however, in the sense that if there is any ambiguity as to particular UK legislation, Convention articles may be referred to as an aid to statutory interpretation (*R* v *Secretary of State for the Home Department, ex parte Brind* (1991); *Anderson* v *HM Advocate* (1996)). Under its international obligations, when the UK ratified the Convention it became bound to adhere to its terms, but the treaty's lack of status as a source of domestic law meant that individuals seeking to assert Convention rights could not do so in the UK domestic courts. Individuals claiming a state abrogation of their human rights were left with the unsavoury option of taking their case to the European Court of Human Rights in Strasbourg (and even this right of petition did not arise until 1966). Such a legal action could entail a long, arduous, expensive and often fruitless journey. So, in this sense, Convention rights in the UK could previously be considered somewhat illusory in nature and difficult to assert in practice.

The legal landscape for those claiming that their human rights have been violated by the state has been radically altered since the enactment of the HRA 1998. The stated purpose of the HRA 1998 was to "bring Convention Rights home". This goal has been achieved to a significant extent by the partial incorporation of the provisions of the articles of the ECHR (and the First and Sixth Protocols) (with the exception of certain derogations and reservations) into domestic law through the HRA 1998. The result is that those seeking to rely on Convention rights may now be able to pursue actions through the domestic courts instead of embarking on a quest to the Strasbourg court. The principal way in which the Convention is incorporated into domestic law is set out in s 6 of the HRA 1998, which stipulates generally that all public bodies must act in accordance with Convention rights. Public bodies include the Scottish Parliament, local authorities, Government Ministers and departments, but, as a sop to the notion of parliamentary supremacy, not the UK Parliament. The HRA 1998 also applies to bodies which, although strictly speaking not public in nature, nevertheless carry out public functions. The Convention rights can thus also apply to wholly private organisations that carry out public functions but only in respect of those public functions and not their private activities. An example of this kind of "quasi-public" body, cited at the time the HRA 1998 was proceeding through the parliamentary process, was "Railtrack" (at that time in the private sector). In respect of its public functions as railway regulator, Railtrack was bound under s 6 to act in accordance with Convention rights; in terms of its private commercial activities, it was not.

In general, s 6 means that an action can be brought by a disaffected member of the public against public (or quasi-public) bodies in respect of an alleged breach of Convention rights even where this does not otherwise infringe the common law of the land. Moreover, given that courts and tribunals are themselves defined as public bodies, they are also bound under s 6 to act in accordance with Convention rights; hence, these rights may also have an impact in relation to all matters determined by courts, including those where there are no public bodies or public functions involved. This is termed the "horizontal effect" of the HRA 1998. There has been some doubt about how far this horizontal effect will extend. For conflicting views see, for example, Sir William Wade (1998) and compare with Lord Justice R Buxton (2000). It seems that the horizontal effect of the HRA 1998 will not supply aggrieved parties with any new grounds of civil action, but the state of existing principles of common law must now be tempered by human rights considerations.

It is also noteworthy that the HRA 1998 is designed in certain ways to take precedence over all other sources of law. For example, by virtue of s 19, prior to the second reading of any UK parliamentary Bill, any Government Minister bringing the proposed legislation to the House must state that in his or her opinion the provisions of the Bill are not contrary to the terms of the ECHR. However, given parliamentary supremacy, UK Acts incompatible with the ECHR are not void: Ministers may proceed with the proposed legislation even though its provisions are not wholly consistent with Convention rights. Court powers of review in this sense are limited merely to declaring that the Act is incompatible. The Minister concerned may rectify the anomaly by a special fast-track procedure but he is not bound to do so. So, in this way, despite the enactment of the HRA 1998, Convention rights are not quite synonymous with a written constitution, the terms of which could not be ignored by Parliament. Nevertheless, where the UK Parliament enacts (or fails to amend) legislation which is contrary to Convention rights, aggrieved individuals would still have the option of taking a case to the Strasbourg court.

As one might expect, matters are somewhat different in respect of legislation of the Scottish Parliament. Under s 31(1) of the Scotland Act 1998, the member of the Scottish Executive responsible for the introduction of any parliamentary Bill must affirm that its provisions do not breach Convention rights. Unlike its UK counterpart, however (as noted above), the Scottish Parliament is forbidden to proceed with legislation which is contrary to Convention rights and any Act passed may be subject to legal challenge on that ground in the Court of Session (Scotland) Act 1998, s 57(2)).

When the HRA 1998 was passed it was shrouded in a great deal of controversy. In particular, a number of commentators voiced concerns that the Act would soon come to be exploited by lawyers either to take issue with the legitimate exercise of public functions or to find loopholes and spurious grounds of action under which their clients could slip through the legal net and avoid criminal liability or civil responsibilities. At the time of writing, human rights issues have begun significantly to influence public activities and judicial decision making. Human rights issues can now be considered an integral part of legal reasoning; and it has been argued that the sorts of reservations concerning the advent of the HRA 1998 outlined above have not come to fruition, by and large (see, for example, K Starmer (2003)). However, the applicability of human rights-based remedies against public organs of the state in the domestic courts has on occasion proved a thorn in policy-makers' sides. Witness, for example, the debacle surrounding the relationship between temporary sheriffs and the Lord Advocate, which triggered a breach of Article 6 of the ECHR (the right to a fair trial) and led to the summary removal of these short-term, stop-gap judges, who in fact had become key in propping up an over-burdened civil justice system (the case is discussed further in Chapter 3). Similarly, the Scottish Executive found both to its own and taxpayers' cost that the somewhat draconian practice of "slopping out" in Scotland's prisons was contrary to the prohibition against inhumane treatment enshrined in the ECHR, which thus gave a right of financial compensation to prisoners. Most recently, a court ruling (in fact in the Strasbourg court) has held that the UK Home Secretary's policy of denying the right to vote to prisoners may be contrary to human rights. Political pressure to enfranchise prisoners seems to be growing – see http://www.guardian.co.uk/society/2008/sep/19/prisonsandprobation.civilliberties.

Common law

The term "common law" in this context stems from the fact that it is law which was originally "common" to the land. As far as Scotland is concerned, such laws evolved from old customary practices, and were often influenced by, and at times imported from, external sources, such as Roman law, Canon law and English law, and were accepted and upheld by the courts in particular cases. Indeed, many areas of Scots law (for example, agency law, criminal law and arbitration) are not principally founded on statutory sources but largely stem from the common law.

Judicial precedent

The role of courts is key in the development of the common law. In this sense, the second major source of Scots law after legislation is the body of principles stemming from court decisions, known as judicial precedent, representing rules which courts have established rather than the law derived from parliamentary action and other legislative forms. Common law develops and becomes a binding source of law primarily by the notion of following previous court decisions (or *stare decisis*). Under this approach courts are generally bound to follow previous decisions of a superior court. Where a prior judgment must be followed, the decision can be termed as "binding". Influential decisions which nevertheless do not require to be followed are known as "persuasive".

It should be noted that judicial precedent is a manifestation of inductive legal reasoning – ie legal principles are induced from individual case decisions. Owing to its deductive heritage (by the influence of Roman law) Scotland did not historically follow a strict system of judicial precedent akin to that which had developed in England. Indeed, many of the Scots institutional writers (see below) expressly rejected this approach. Principally caused by an increase in case reporting, and arguably the influence of the English-dominated House of Lords (sitting as a court), in the 18th century Scotland gradually adopted a more rigid system of judicial precedent. In 1828 the Court of Session accepted that a prior decision of the court was binding.

Binding decisions. As mentioned above, court decisions are generally binding only when made by a superior court. Moreover, the present case must relate to the same point of law as dealt with by the previous court. Both these issues are now explored in more detail.

The civil court hierarchy (The Scottish court structure is discussed in detail in Chapter 3.)

In terms of the civil court hierarchy, the ECJ sits at the top and its decisions (pertaining to interpretations of EC law) bind all courts in the UK, although it is not bound by its own previous decisions.

The House of Lords (sitting as a court) will set precedents for Scotland only in relation to appeals deriving from the Scottish courts or those cases dealing with the interpretation of UK statutes that apply in Scotland. Again, in similarity to the ECJ, the House of Lords may choose not to follow its own previous decisions.

The Court of Session is divided into the Outer House (a court of "first instance") and the Inner House (principally an appeal court). The decisions of the Inner House bind both itself and the Outer House and the inferior sheriff courts. Where a decision has been reached by one Inner House division, however, it may be overturned by a "full bench" of seven Inner House judges. Principally because they represent the view of a single judge, Outer House and sheriff court judgments are never binding; they may, however, be persuasive. (The Court of Session is discussed in more detail in Chapter 3.)

The criminal court hierarchy. Judicial precedent is not so rigidly adhered to in the Scottish criminal courts. For example, the High Court of Justiciary, when sitting as an appeal court, is able to depart from its own previous decisions. Sheriff courts are bound to follow decisions of the High Court sitting as an appeal court. Moreover, sheriff courts are likely to view decisions of single judges made at first instance in the High Court with respect and, in practice, will generally adhere thereto, even though it would seem that they are not formally bound to do so.

Cases to be in point. Before a court is bound to adhere to a former decision, it must be dealing with the same point of law as the previous case. This can be termed as being "in point" or "on all fours". When a case is in point it may be factually quite different to the previous case but the fundamental issue is whether it concerns the same point of law that the decision in the previous case turned upon – ie the point of law (such as a common law principle of contract law, or a particular interpretation of a provision in a statute) the determination of which will decide how the case ought to be resolved. This point of law can be termed the *ratio decidendi* or simply the *ratio*. It is only the *ratio* of a case that is binding.

Determining the *ratio* of a case may be an art in itself. In particular, it may be hard to prise the *ratio* from all other aspects of the case debated by the court. It could be argued that some judges like to pontificate at length and in any judgment the court may embark on a long and, at times, arduous journey into the various legal matters holding some relevance to the case at hand. Many hypothetical matters, historical issues and ancillary legal points may be raised, debated and examined in fine detail by the judges. All such other remarks and opinions made in the court's judgment, which fall outwith the true *ratio* of the case, may be termed *obiter dicta* or *obiter*. *Obiter* remarks are never binding as such but they may be highly persuasive, particularly when made by a senior court.

Decisions of foreign courts. In novel situations where Scots law sources are deficient, courts may have recourse to decisions taken by foreign courts. In particular, English decisions may be influential, especially in legal spheres where the law is broadly similar across the UK (such as commercial and industrial law). As mentioned in Chapter 1, English law has been the cornerstone of a host of legal systems across the globe, including many US states and Commonwealth countries; therefore, decisions of the courts and statutory rules in these jurisdictions may also be of relevance from time to time. The Scottish courts may also examine other sources of the rules and principles of foreign legal systems (for example, legislation or legal writings) when Scots law does not provide a solution. In particular, reference to legal writings on Roman law (historically influential on Scots law), may be of import, albeit that the influence of Roman sources has dwindled in more modern times.

Case reports. Clearly, if judicial precedent is to function then previous decisions and judgments require to be recorded and capable of being found and cited by the parties and scrutinised by courts in subsequent cases. Beginning in Scotland with the development of "practicks" – early notes on cases first made in the time of James V – different case reporting series have become ever more common in modern times. In Scotland a number of different case reporting series may be referred to by parties in the hope of finding precedents that will assist their legal case. The most authoritative series of Scottish case reports is *Session Cases* which reports decisions (and judgments) of the Court of Session and Scottish appeals to the House of Lords. Other reports include *Scottish Criminal Case Reports*, *Scottish Civil Law Reports*, *Greens Weekly Digest* and *Scots Law Times*. In terms of finding cases, readers should note that court decisions are commonly (but not always) cited using the names of the parties, the year, the case reporting series and the page number at which the case can be found. So, for example, in *Woolfson* v *Strathclyde Regional Council* (1978), the parties to the action were Woolfson and Strathclyde Regional Council; the year of the case, 1978; the case reporting series, *Session Cases* (denoted by "SC") and the page number 84.

Many case reports are now accessible on-line via legal research packages such as Westlaw or LexisNexis. Students and practitioners alike can now avoid ploughing through dusty tomes in their law libraries and instead search across different case reporting volumes at the stroke of a key, which has made legal research a far less onerous process and aided the development of the law through precedent in a number of areas.

Precedent: advantages and drawbacks. The system of judicial precedent fulfils a number of important functions. Principally speaking, judicial precedent promotes certainty and fairness in the law. Without a system of precedent, the law would in general be more ambiguous and it is likely that more court actions would be brought in the face of conflicting views on the state of the law. Previous decided cases give disputing parties guidance on the respective strengths of their legal cases – often a reality check which limits litigation.

Judicial precedent is also fundamentally bound up with the principle of natural justice – in particular, the notion that the law should be applied in the same way to all within society. Related to this is the idea that the lower courts are less likely to make errors in their interpretation of the law if they are handed down guidance through precedents from the superior courts. It seems logical that more junior judges should benefit from the experience and skill of their more senior colleagues. Linked to this is the idea that judicial precedent limits arbitrariness – ie the ability of the judge to deviate from recognised legal norms and impose his or her own subjective view as to what a particular legal principle should entail. Judicial precedent also allows the law to develop incrementally in a uniform and logical manner given that courts can apply and amplify recognised legal principles to meet novel scenarios. So, in this sense, the courts may fill gaps in the law until Parliament determines to intervene.

As a system, however, judicial precedent does have its drawbacks. Law may become too rigid and inflexible if courts become restrained by previous decisions, which arguably either were wrongly decided or are no longer relevant. As a pertinent example, laws which served to render a husband immune from any charge that he had raped his wife were arguably preserved by the system of judicial precedent at a time when social standards had shifted in such a way as to hold the rule wholly unacceptable.

Judicial precedent is not, in practice, always followed. For example, in an attempt to avoid the impact of a previous, perhaps unpopular, decision, the court may strive to split hairs and find artificial distinctions with a previous decision that would normally be considered binding. More fundamentally, it may not always be an easy task to ascertain the *ratio* of any particular case. In reaching a decision, judges may follow two or more legal principles in determining their decision, or in some cases (particularly found in old, sketchy judgments) perhaps no discernible legal rationale at all! In appeal cases, where there is more than one judge sitting, different judges may be in accordance with each other but arrive at the same decision by different legal journeys, deploying different *ratios*.

Finally, it should be noted that many judgments still in fact remain unreported. Thus, many precedents go unnoticed. This is somewhat unsatisfactory. The lack of a universal system of reporting leads to a haphazard system of legal development. Moreover, in practice, finding a precedent that might support one's case may become no more than a random, luck-of-the-draw activity.

Institutional writers

As noted in Chapter 1, the works of the institutional writers, eminent legal jurists, beginning in the late 17th century and continuing through to the early 19th century, were instrumental in charting the development of a maturing Scottish legal system. The works provided comprehensive discussions of various tracts of Scots law and laid the foundations for modern Scots law in a number of areas. The works drew upon early decisions of the Scottish courts, Scottish customary practices, general principles of morality and reason and the laws of other jurisdictions including Roman law, Canon law and English law. The writings were so revered that they began to be considered as formal sources of Scots law in themselves.

With the exponential rise in legislation seen over recent years, coupled with the adoption of a strict system of judicial precedent and comprehensive case reporting systems, the importance of institutional works as a formal source of law has diminished greatly. However, if the law is otherwise found wanting, then a principle expounded by an institutional writer may be considered as a valid source of law and may be cited in court as such. Institutional works are primarily of historical interest, especially in establishing the origins of many areas of Scots law and in determining how the Scots legal system has been influenced by other schools of legal thinking.

The first institutional writing was Sir Thomas Craig's discussion of property law in the *Jus Feudale* of 1655. The most influential and important work, however, was penned by Viscount Stair (James Dalrymple). His *Institutions of Scots Law*, first published in 1681, can be seen as the cornerstone upon which much of Scots law was built. This monumental work spanned a wide array of areas of Scots law including that relating to obligations, property and succession.

Other important institutional writings include:

- Sir George Mackenzie, *The Laws and Customs of Scotland in Matters Criminal* (1678)

- Lord Bankton, *An Institute of the Laws of Scotland* (1751–53)
- Professor John Erskine, *An Institute of the Laws of Scotland* (1773)
- Baron David Hume, *Commentaries on the Law of Scotland respecting Crimes* (1797)
- Professor George Bell, *Commentaries on the law of Scotland and on the Principles of Mercantile Jurisprudence* (1810); *Principles of the Law of Scotland* (1829).

Modern writings. Textbooks, articles and other pieces of legal writing have become increasingly common over recent years. Generally speaking, these kinds of non-institutional works cannot be said to represent formal legal sources of law; rather, they merely represent an author's opinion on particular aspects of the law. Despite this, in modern times, some of the more esteemed legal works are cited in court both by parties' legal representatives and also by judges. Non-institutional works are only ever considered to be persuasive. Opinions of writers in influential texts may gain a legal authority but such authority will merely stem from the fact that the court has approved that viewpoint. It is therefore the court's view that is the authority, not, strictly speaking, the opinion of the writer.

Custom

As noted in Chapter 1, custom was an important way in which, historically speaking, Scots common law developed. It is possible that a custom can still be identified and viewed as a formal source of new law. In modern times this is something of a rarity given that many customary practices have been assimilated into law either by court decisions or through legislation. Nevertheless, a custom may be recognised as a new source of law if it can be shown to have been acquiesced in for a substantial period of time; where it is well defined and certain; if fair and reasonable; and if not inconsistent with recognised principles of law. One well-known case in which a party attempted to rely upon a custom as a valid source of law was *Bruce* v *Smith* (1890), where the owner of property adjacent to waters in which whaling took place claimed to hold a customary right to a share in the spoils of such activities. In this case, however, the test of reasonableness failed and the custom was held not to represent the law.

Additionally, customary practices may bestow legal rights to parties in individual cases. In business contracts, for example, commonly accepted customs and practices of trade may be implied into these agreements, in the absence of any express reference thereto. For this to occur the customary rule must be widely accepted within the trade, specific, reasonable and not overruled by any express terms of the contract. A recent case in which a customary practice was held to be incorporated into a contract in this way is *Stirling Park & Co* v *Digby Brown & Co* (1995) in which it was held that, by custom of trade, solicitors would become personally liable for certain fees owing to sheriff officers, if their client failed to make the payment due.

Customary rights can also be seen within the sphere of land law: what can be termed as "public rights of way" may arise, whereby members of the public may gain a customary right to walk across a piece of private land.

Equity

While any modern society would hope that the notion of equity or fairness would be at the very heart of its laws, equity has a particular meaning as a source of law in itself. It should be noted that the Scottish legal system differs in this sense, from the English. In view of its somewhat rigid early legal system, England historically developed a separate and distinct system of equity (overseen by the Chancery Court to deal with equitable claims, where the law did not provide a remedy). Law and equity were never split in this manner in Scotland. For Scotland, equity in practice represents a mechanism by which harsher facets of the law can be softened. So, for example, Scottish courts developed equitable court remedies to be granted to parties in deserving cases, including those of specific implement (an order to carry out a particular act) and interdict (an order prohibiting a particular act).

In addition, the superior courts in Scotland (the Court of Session and the High Court of Justiciary) may have recourse to the *nobile officium* (literally, "equitable power"). The *nobile officium* allows the court (albeit rarely) to grant a remedy, remove the entitlement to enforce a particular legal right, or deem a particular act a criminal one, where it determines that it is equitable to do so, even where, strictly speaking, the law does not. One of the best-known applications of the *nobile officium* occurred in *Khaliq* v *HM Advocate* (1984) in which a shopkeeper was held guilty of selling kits designed for "glue-sniffing" to children. Although this conduct did not amount to an offence under the existing criminal law of Scotland, the High Court of Justiciary exercised its equitable power to render the act criminal in the interests of public safety. While such judicial activism is rare, the *nobile officium* can be said to represent a (limited) law-making function within the courts.

QUASI-SOURCES OF LAW

Codes of practice are examples of "quasi-sources" of law – ie rules and principles which are not themselves law but are connected with the enforcement of law, may appear like law and are sometimes treated as such. Such codes are generally brief, systematic and reasonably comprehensive sets of precepts produced by government or public regulator and are targeted to the public or a particular industry. They may be produced to encourage a particular activity to be carried out more safely or more effectively in some way and tend to be written in a plain, understandable fashion rather than being littered with legal jargon. Codes may be required or permitted by an Act of Parliament and sometimes require parliamentary approval.

Codes have varying levels of enforceability. Some codes offer mere guidance and are not enforceable in any way – eg the Secretary of State's guidance in respect of the Transport Act 1985, s 125, in relation to the needs of disabled persons. Others are indirectly enforceable in certain ways. For example, ss 16 and 17 of the Health and Safety at Work etc Act 1974 empower the Health and Safety Commission (subject to the approval of the Secretary of State) to approve and/or issue codes of practice which it regards as suitable to provide guidance on the application of the Act and regulations made under the Act. By virtue of s 17, failure to observe the codes shall not render that person liable to criminal or civil proceedings. If a criminal offence is alleged, however, any approved code may be cited in evidence. Furthermore, where there is a failure to comply with the code, an accused person may be required to illustrate that he adhered to the objectives of the code in a manner other than implementing the code. Similarly, in civil proceedings it appears that a failure to comply with the code may be used in evidence to support a civil case where negligence is alleged.

Essential Facts

- Sources may denote historical, philosophical or formal sources of law.
- The term "formal source" refers to the way in which a particular rule becomes binding.
- The formal sources can be divided into statutory sources; and common law sources, including judicial precedent, institutional writings, custom and equity.

- The primary source of Scots law is legislation. There is a range of bodies now empowered to legislate for the people of Scotland, including the UK Parliament, the EU, the Scottish Parliament, and many bodies and individuals delegated the right to legislate.

- The UK Parliament is composed of two chambers: the elected House of Commons; and the non-elected House of Lords. The House of Lords is currently undergoing a period of reform.

- Given that the UK is a parliamentary democracy, the UK Parliament is the supreme legislative body. However, power has been voluntarily conceded (or devolved) to other bodies.

- The UK parliamentary process is a complex, drawn-out process involving both chambers of the House. Royal Assent of the monarch is required before an Act can become law. The bulk of legislation is promoted by the Government in the House of Commons.

- The Scotland Act 1998 led to the inception of the Scottish Parliament which is empowered to enact laws in "devolved areas". Many more important policy issues have been "reserved to Westminster".

- Delegated legislation may be subject to both internal control within either the UK or Scottish Parliament and external control through the courts, although it has been argued that neither is generally effective in practice. The key test of delegated legislation is its legality.

- In modern times EC legislation has become a major source of Scots law. In general it has dominance over domestic provisions of Scots law.

- While the primary sources of EC law are found in treaties, secondary EC law is made by an interactive process between the European Commission, Council of Ministers and European Parliament.

- EC law may take a number of forms including regulations, directives and decisions. While regulations and decisions generally have direct effect, directives normally do not and require to be brought into domestic law before they are enforceable in Scotland.

- Statutory interpretation is the process by which courts or a lawyer interpret statutory provisions and apply them to a given set of facts. Courts may take different approaches in this respect including the literal rule, the liberal rule, the golden rule and the mischief rule.

- The ECHR sets out a number of fundamental rights and freedoms. The ECHR is not, generally speaking, a formal source of Scots law but has been partially incorporated into domestic law by the Human Rights

Act 1998. Scottish citizens can now generally enforce the terms of the Convention through the domestic courts against public bodies.

- Court decisions operate as a source of common law by way of judicial precedent which holds that the decisions of superior courts become binding on inferior courts.

- A previous judgment will be binding only if the *ratio decidendi*, ie the legal principle upon which that case was decided, is the same as the *ratio* in the present case. All other matters referred to in the judgment are know as *obiter dicta* and are not binding

- Institutional writers produced works mapping out different areas of Scots law as it developed historically. Such works were historically important formal sources of law. They are of lesser importance now, given the modern impact of judicial precedent and legislation.

- A custom may be recognised as a source of new law where it is well established; recognised and practised; well defined and certain; fair and reasonable; and not contrary to established legal principles.

- Equity is a method by which the law can be softened in practice. Courts have developed the equitable remedies of "specific implement" and "interdict"; and the superior Scottish courts have a limited power of *nobile officium* which allows them either to grant or deny a remedy, or hold that a particular act is a criminal one even if this does not, strictly speaking, represent the law.

- Quasi-sources of law include codes of practice which, although looking like law and often treated as such, merely represent embellishments on or explanations as to how laws can be applied in practice. They have varying levels of enforceability.

Essential Cases

A v Scottish Ministers (2001): rare example of challenge to a Scottish Parliamentary Act after receiving Royal Assent; Act was made retrospective and was challenged by judicial review on human rights basis; action failed on basis that human rights complained about were not absolute and could be abrogated by the state in the interests of public safety.

Litster v Forth Dry Dock Co (1989): in terms of EC law's validity as a source of law, House of Lords was willing to write into domestic provisions words not approved by Parliament in order to give effect to provisions of the directive concerned.

Marshall v Southampton and South-West Hampshire Area Health Authority (1986): female employee, forced to retire aged 62, claimed that employer health authority was acting in a discriminatory fashion contrary to Article 119 of EC Treaty and Equal Treatment Directive 76/207; the authority was a public body, so it was bound to act within terms of the directive, even though its terms had not been enacted into domestic law.

Eddington v Robertson (1895): wife was entitled under common law to share of husband's moveable estate if he died or divorced her; put on statutory footing by Married Women's Property (Scotland) Act 1881, although under Act this share in estate available only when husband died; although absence of statutory right to share in estate on divorce almost certainly caused by draftsman's slip, court adopted a literal rule and refused to amend wording to grant divorced wife a remedy.

Adler v George (1964): adopting the golden rule, literal statutory wording which read "in the vicinity of" interpreted to include actions committed by defendant in case that took place within area concerned, and not, strictly speaking, within its vicinity.

Bruce v Smith (1890): owner of property adjacent to waters in which whaling took place sought to assert customary right to share in spoils of such activities; test of reasonableness failed; custom did not represent the law.

Khaliq v HM Advocate (1984): shopkeeper guilty of selling kits designed for "glue-sniffing" to children; although conduct did not amount to offence under existing criminal law of Scotland, High Court of Justiciary exercised *nobile officium* to render act criminal in interests of public safety.

3 THE SCOTTISH JUDICIAL SYSTEM

This chapter provides a discussion of the Scottish judicial system including an overview of its workings, procedures, remedies, sanctions and enforcement mechanisms. Prior to embarking on a detailed examination of different courts, it may first be useful to consider a number of fundamental issues about the judicial system in general.

In most modern systems of law there are, fundamentally, two types of court: the civil court and the criminal court. Civil courts are provided by the state and act as a forum in which disputes over the civil law (ie non-criminal law issues) may be resolved. Civil courts can be seen as an avenue of last resort if parties find themselves unable to find a solution to their dispute by consensual means. Generally one party is seeking to enforce a legal right in some way against another and will be seeking a specified remedy from the court. In any litigation through the courts, the party raising the action is termed the "pursuer", and the party defending the action is known as the "defender". While commonly the civil courts arbitrate disputes between two private individuals, at times the state may also be a party, whether acting as pursuer or defender. In plain terms, after hearing both legal arguments and factual assertions from both parties, the court will rule in favour of one or other of the parties and either grant the remedy sought or deny that remedy.

Criminal courts are also provided by the state. Unlike civil courts, in which proceedings are generally instigated by private parties, the criminal courts represent fora in which the state is able to raise legal proceedings against members of the public. Such an action, known as a "prosecution", may be raised against those alleged to have acted in a manner contrary to the criminal law of the land. As noted in Chapter 1, the criminal law sets down a minimum moral code or standard of behaviour required by the state. Any "accused" person may be judged or "tried" accordingly in the criminal courts.

If an accused is found guilty of a crime, he may be punished (or "sentenced") accordingly (sentencing is discussed in more detail below). There are in fact three verdicts which can be passed against an accused person by a criminal court: "guilty"; "not guilty;" and "not proven". The "not proven" verdict, which will lead to the acquittal of the accused, has long been a controversial one, criticised as being ill-defined and unsatisfactory. In fact, if one examines the criminal court process in a strict fashion then it is perhaps the "not guilty" verdict that is an illogical one. In criminal cases, the prosecution must attempt to prove the guilt of the offender – there is no correlative duty imposed upon the defence to prove the innocence of the accused. In strict terms, the only question is then whether or not guilt has been proven or not proven. If the guilt is not established, it does not necessarily follow that the accused is not guilty, except perhaps in the sense that one is deemed innocent until proven guilty under the law.

In both civil and criminal courts, the procedure is "adversarial". What this entails is that the parties must bring forth arguments of both fact and law. Each party, therefore, presents evidence of his (perhaps partisan) view of the facts of the case and also sets forth legal arguments based on his interpretation of particular rules of law that are central to and aid the case he seeks to present (for example, legislative sources or principles of common law). In general, unlike the case in inquisitorial court systems found, for example, in continental Europe, there is no independent inquiry into the facts and law carried out by the judge.

Determinations of the relevant law that will apply to the case, such as statutory interpretation or application of established judicial precedent, are made by the presiding judge. Factual issues may in some cases also be determined by the judge, but in other cases – primarily in more serious criminal matters – the facts of the case are established by a jury of members of the public. These issues are discussed in more detail below.

One of the key differences between civil and criminal courts is the standard of proof required in each. For a finding of guilt to be held against an accused in a criminal action, the case must be proved against him "beyond all reasonable doubt", whereas in a civil action the standard of proof by which the court must find to rule in favour of one party over another is the lesser standard of "on the balance of probabilities". Similarly, there are different rules relating to the nature of evidence in both – the key one being that in a criminal case all essential facts require to be corroborated (ie drawn from two or more independent sources), whereas there is no requirement for corroboration of evidence in civil matters.

THE CIVIL COURTS

Civil jurisdiction

As a primary rule, a court can only determine any action brought before it when it has jurisdiction. Jurisdiction must be held both in respect of the type of case brought before the court and also in relation to the parties to the action. In this latter sense, the court must hold jurisdiction over the defender, under the doctrine *actor sequitur forum rei* (the pursuer is bound to "follow the court of the defender"). Jurisdictional issues will be discussed further when examining the different civil courts below.

There are three principal civil courts that hold jurisdiction in Scotland:

• the sheriff court
• the Court of Session
• the Judicial Committee of the House of Lords (although it should be noted that, at the time of writing, the jurisdiction of this court over Scottish civil matters is set to be removed and replaced by a new "Supreme Court", which is discussed further below).

Sheriff courts

Sheriff courts are prevalent throughout Scotland. In terms of their organisational structure, sheriff court business is split into six geographical areas known as "sheriffdoms". Based upon old, regional local government areas, the six sheriffdoms are: Grampian, Highland and Islands; Tayside, Central and Fife; Lothian and Borders; Glasgow and Strathkelvin; North Strathclyde; and South Strathclyde, Dumfries and Galloway. The sheriffdoms are in turn split into a total of 49 sheriff court districts. Within each sheriff court district can be found a sheriff court and a number of sheriffs. Sheriff court business within each sheriffdom is organised and administered by a head sheriff, termed a "sheriff principal". As alluded to further below, the sheriff principal also acts as an appeal judge and may hear civil cases appealed from sheriff court decisions.

Sheriffs principal and sheriffs are theoretically appointed by the monarch. In practice, however, the Queen acts on the recommendation of the First Minister, who is in turn bound to consult with the Lord President (Scotland Act 1998, s 95(4)). Sheriffs must be solicitors or advocates of at least 10 years' standing (Sheriff Courts (Scotland) Act 1971, s 5). The sheriff principal is also vested with a right to appoint honorary sheriffs (Sheriff Courts (Scotland) Act 1907). These special kinds of sheriff are not generally legally qualified and in practice seldom sit in court. The Lord Advocate (a member of the Scottish Executive and Head of the Prosecution Service in Scotland) was formerly empowered to provide advice to the Secretary of State for Scotland in respect of the appointment of temporary sheriffs as and when required to ease the workload of the sheriff courts. In the aftermath of a landmark court ruling (*Starrs* v *Ruxton* (2000)), however, temporary sheriffs were abolished. The rationale behind this decision was essentially that the control over temporary sheriffs' appointment and re-appointment exercised by the Lord Advocate (as the head of the prosecution service) was deemed contrary to the right to a fair trial enshrined in Article 6 of the European Convention on Human Rights. It was argued that, as re-appointment was in practice at the whim of the Lord Advocate, this might potentially lead to temporary sheriffs acting in such a way as to curry his favour. An additional 12 full-time and a large number of part-time shrieval appointments were made in order to cover the shortfall in judicial manpower that resulted from the abolition of temporary sheriffs, who, although initially employed as a "stop-gap", had over time become an integral cog in the Scottish civil justice machine.

Sheriff court jurisdiction

(i) Jurisdiction over the defender. Sheriff court jurisdiction over defenders can occur in different ways. In general, jurisdiction is governed under the Sheriff Courts (Scotland) Act 1907 and the Civil Jurisdiction and Judgments Act 1982 (as amended by the Civil Jurisdiction and Amendments Order 2001). The court will hold jurisdiction over the defender where he:

- lives in the sheriffdom (for at least 40 days, or has ceased to reside there for less than 40 days and has no known address within Scotland. Alternatively, if of no fixed abode, the defender may be "personally cited" to appear in the court); or
- carries on business in the sheriffdom (in which case he may be cited at his place of business); or
- owns, or is the tenant of, land or buildings within the sheriffdom, if the action is connected with the property owned; or
- is involved in a contractual dispute where the contract was to be performed in the sheriffdom or the action relates to a delict (a civil legal wrong) which took place in the sheriffdom.

(ii) Jurisdiction over subject-matter. The sheriff court can hear civil cases of all kinds, aside from a small category of claims that must be taken to the superior Court of Session and cases in particular dispute areas that require to be raised in tribunals and other specialist courts. Additionally, the sheriff court holds exclusive (or "privative") jurisdiction over particular cases.

Sheriff court procedures. Depending on the type of case being brought, the pursuer must bring one of three types of claim: the "small claim"; the "summary cause"; or the "ordinary cause".

Small claims. At the bottom of the jurisdictional rung is the small claims procedure (which is technically a species of the summary cause). Introduced under the Law Reform (Miscellaneous Provisions) (Scotland) Act 1985, a small claim must be brought where the monetary value of the claim is below

£3,000. It is worth noting, however, that sheriffs may decide to convert a small claim into a summary cause or an ordinary cause (see below) if of the opinion that there are complex questions of law involved or where a joint motion of the parties makes such a request under the Law Reform (Miscellaneous Provisions) (Scotland) Act 1990.

The small claim procedure is the most truncated and (at least in theory) informal. For example, some of the strict legal rules pertaining to the admissibility of evidence which apply to other court proceedings are relaxed. The idea of the small claim is that the informality of the proceedings will mean that the process will be both speedy and cost-effective, with the parties not requiring lawyers and hence saving on legal costs. No legal aid (state-provided financial assistance to engage a lawyer) is hence available in small claims. It is worth noting that it has been argued for some time that small claims are not always run in an informal fashion and may in practice mirror judicial proceedings in other civil courts (see Mays and Clark, "ADR and the Courts" (1997) 2 SLPQ 57).

It costs between £6 and £35 to raise a small claim. Legal expense claims to recoup these and associated costs are kept to a minimum. Scotland (as well as England) generally operates a "loser pays" rule in civil legal proceedings. In this respect, the maximum that can be claimed is £150 where the value of the claim is between £200 and £1,500; 10 per cent of the claim value where the claim is between £1,500 and £3,000; and zero where the claim is less than £200.

Summary cause. The summary cause procedure is governed by the Sheriff Courts (Scotland) Act 1971 (although the latest rules were put in place in 2002). A summary cause must be raised where the monetary value sought is between £3,000 and £5,000 and also for actions pertaining to eviction from heritable property.

Reflecting the limited importance of the types of action brought thereunder, the summary cause, as its name suggests, is a shortened form of court process, where some of the general strict court procedural rules are relaxed. Actions may be raised by the pursuer completing a pre-printed claim form. If the defender does not return the form by a particular date (known as the "return day") the court will automatically grant a decree in favour of the pursuer (although actions relating to eviction from heritable property do not have return days). Where the claim is timeously defended then a trial date (known as a "proof") is set for a subsequent date (for a detailed examination of summary cause procedure, see D Auchie (2004)).

In a similar vein to small claims, a summary cause must be treated as an ordinary cause procedure where both parties submit a motion to this effect to the court. In other cases, for example, where one party submits a motion, or in relation to actions regarding the recovery of possession of property, the sheriff will have discretion in deciding whether that case should be heard by an ordinary cause.

Ordinary cause. Any other civil court action brought in the sheriff court is raised as an "ordinary cause". The court procedure inherent in the ordinary cause is provided for by the Sheriff Courts (Scotland) Act 1907 and represents the most formal, complex and hence (in practice) most costly in the sheriff court. An ordinary cause is brought by the lodging of a document termed an "initial writ", which maps out the pursuer's grounds of claim in both legal and factual assertions. Where an action is to be defended, the initial writ is met by a set of answers known as "defences" lodged by the defender. What follows is a negotiation period in which "adjustments" to the legal and factual issues in dispute can be made by the parties, which might include admissions from either side and agreements on certain matters arrived at between the disputing parties. Any remaining grounds of dispute are determined at an "options" hearing where the future procedure for resolving the dispute is set out. If necessary, the matter may proceed to trial ("proof") before the court.

Sheriff court appeals. Parties dissatisfied with decisions made by sheriffs may, depending on the type of action, have recourse to a right of appeal. Given the limited value sought in a small claim, appeal is available to the sheriff principal on a point of law only, by a procedure termed "stated case", in which the sheriff states his case – ie the reasons for his decision – to the sheriff principal. The same appeal procedure applies in a summary cause. A further appeal from the sheriff principal may be taken to the Inner House of the Court of Session where leave to do so is granted. Similar rights of appeal from ordinary cause decisions can be made. In an ordinary cause, however, an appeal can be made directly to the Inner Court of Session.

The Court of Session

The Court of Session sits permanently in Edinburgh. The court is divided into two "Houses": the "Outer House", a court of the first instance in which cases may be raised for the first time; and the "Inner House", primarily an appeal court. As noted in Chapter 1, the Court of Session, as Scotland's first permanent court, is an institution with a significant history, established back in 1532. The Court has seen radical reform over the years, although its present composition was largely established in the early 19th century and its current procedures are principally regulated by the Court of Session Act 1988.

Court of Session jurisdiction

Jurisdiction over the defender. Jurisdictional issues are largely governed by the Civil Jurisdiction and Judgments Act 1982. Unlike the situation as regards sheriff courts, the Court of Session holds jurisdiction over the whole of Scotland. The court follows the general rule as regards jurisdiction in that the key issue is that the court holds some authority over the defender. The principal method by which jurisdiction is founded over a defender is that he is permanently or habitually resident in Scotland. If this is not possible, jurisdiction may be claimed on the basis that the defender is the tenant or owner of heritable property in Scotland (it is not necessary for the action to relate to that property).

Particular jurisdictional rules arise in respect of consistorial matters: eg matrimonial actions such as divorce, legal separation and nullity of marriage. In such instances, the court may exert jurisdiction when either party to the marriage in question has a permanent home in Scotland on the date the action commenced, or was habitually resident in Scotland for one year immediately prior to the commencement of proceedings.

Jurisdiction over subject-matter. As noted above, certain cases (eg those where the monetary value of the claim is £5,000 or less) must be raised in the appropriate sheriff court. The sheriff court was given a concurrent jurisdiction to hear divorce cases in 1984 but a small category of cases remain that must be raised in the Court of Session, including those relating to personal status, actions of reduction, actions relating to the tenor of lost documents and judicial review petitions. Moreover, where a party seeks recourse to the court's *nobile officium* ("equitable power") in civil matters this is only available in the Court of Session.

There is significant overlap as regards the jurisdiction of the sheriff court and of the Court of Session respectively. In the bulk of civil cases a pursuer is at liberty to choose between raising an action in the Court of Session and raising it in the local sheriff court. In cases which are of greater importance legally or financially, the Court of Session may be the more attractive option as this court has a higher legal status, which may mean that its decisions are less likely to be appealed. On the downside, however, given the generally more protracted nature of Court of Session procedures (although it should be noted that procedural matters have been improved of late), litigation is likely to incur more time and greater costs than an equivalent action in the sheriff court. In addition, parties will be required to attend the court in Edinburgh at particular stages of the litigation process, which may be less convenient than attending a local sheriff court. Moreover, litigants will be required to engage advocates or solicitor-advocates in addition to solicitors to represent them in the Court of Session, substantially increasing the financial burden of the action.

The Outer House. Cases in the Outer House are heard by a single judge, known as a "Lord Ordinary", who generally sits alone with no jury. Juries in civil trials have been largely abolished and are now entirely absent from civil sheriff court proceedings; but a remnant of the past may be found in industrial accidents claims in the Outer House where a jury of 12 may sit to deliberate over the facts of the case. Although recruitment to the judiciary is examined elsewhere in this book, it is worth noting here that Lords Ordinary are former legal practitioners: either suitably experienced Queen's Counsel (QCs), former sheriffs of 5 years' standing or solicitor-advocates of 5 years' standing. In recent times the number of judges has increased to help shore up the somewhat creaking Scottish civil justice system. At the time of writing there are 24 Outer House judges in the Court of session (see http://www. scotcourts.gov.uk/session/index.asp).

Outer House procedure. Civil actions in the Outer House are normally commenced by one party lodging a written "summons" mapping out the principal legal and factual grounds of claim. If the other party to the case seeks to defend the action then this is done by the lodging of a corresponding set of "defences". In a similar process to that found in the sheriff court ordinary cause, the parties then enter into a period in which they will adjust the pleadings between them and the grounds of dispute may be refined and narrowed, known as the "open record". When adjustments come to an end the record is said to be "closed". The case may then proceed to a proof (a trial to determine the facts of the case) or else a hearing may be held to determine certain legal issues which require to be resolved prior to proof. Additionally, there may be other occasions in which the court is required to ascertain particular facts of the case before it can proceed to legal argument. This kind of hearing is known as a "proof before answer".

In addition, certain actions are brought by "petition". In basic terms, such actions (eg for the court to appoint new trustees or wind up a company or partnership) are brought by one party (the "petitioner") petitioning the court for a particular remedy that only the court can grant. The court may, where appropriate, remit the petition to a suitably qualified third party to determine the merits of the case sought and report back to the court. In particular instances, such as the seeking of a remedy sought by a minority (shareholding) party in a company against the majority shareholders, the petition may be contentious and, in this type of case, on receipt of the petition, the court may determine which parties should receive notice of it. Such parties, known as the "respondents", may then have the option of defending the petition in court.

Appeals from the Outer House. Decisions of the Outer House may be appealed to the Inner House by what is known as a "reclaiming motion". Appeals are normally made on a point of law, although rarely an appeal may be heard on the facts. The appeal procedure is discussed further below.

The Inner House. The Inner House is in essence an appeal court, although it has a small "first instance" jurisdiction to provide litigants with interpretations on points of law (eg taxation cases and certain petitions by limited companies). The Inner House hears appeals from the Outer House, sheriff courts and other tribunals. There are two divisions in the Inner House: the First Division, comprising the Lord President (Scotland's senior judge) and four other judges known as "Lords of Session"; and the Second Division, comprising the Lord Justice-Clerk (depute to the Lord President) and five Lords of Session. In hearing any appeal either division may sit and normally three judges will be present without any jury. In matters of particular import the court may sit as a "full bench" of seven judges. This number may also be expanded by including further judges from the Outer House. In busier times an Extra Division of Outer House judges may be convened to help expedite business through the Inner House.

Inner House procedure. As noted above, appeals on the facts of cases are rare. The court is normally concerned with hearing arguments over disputed points of law (such as an interpretation of a statutory provision, or common law doctrine) which determined how the decision of the previous court was arrived at. After hearing an appeal, judges may deliver an instant decision orally or, more commonly, may adjourn the hearing (known as "making *avizandum*") and issue a written opinion at some later date. In practice it is common for one of the judges to deliver an extensive, detailed opinion. Commonly, the other judges will simply issue supplementary, "concurring" judgments, which may merely stipulate that the judge has had the opportunity to read his colleague's opinion and is in agreement with it. With decisions taken by majority, judges are sometimes in disagreement, however. In such a case, a judge may issue a "dissenting" opinion. The decision of the court may be either to dismiss the appeal by "adhering" to the decision of the trial judge or, alternatively, to uphold the appeal by "recalling" the decision of the trial judge and substituting a new one.

Appeals from the Inner House. Parties unhappy with the decision or "interlocutor" issued by the Inner House may have a further right of appeal to the Judicial Committee of the House of Lords. This procedure, which is generally available only on a point of law, follows upon a petition "praying" that the Lords reverse the previous decision. Generally this right arises only when the Court of Session grants leave to appeal. Leave is not required where the Inner House decision is not unanimous.

Judicial Committee of the House of Lords

The House of Lords in its judicial capacity is not synonymous with the second legislative chamber of the UK Parliament. As a court, only the "judicial committee" of the House sits, comprising the Lord Chancellor and number of "Lords of Appeal in Ordinary". These eminent law lords will either have held high judicial office or be barristers or advocates of at least 15 years' standing (but, in practice, generally for a much longer period).

Although traditionally an English-based court, the House of Lords may hear appeals from the Scottish civil courts. Despite controversy regarding the legal basis of this practice, the right of appeal to the Lords was first established in *Greenshields* v *Magistrates of Edinburgh* (1710–11). There is no concurrent jurisdiction in Scottish criminal matters. A significant criticism of the system, however, is that although the judicial committee by convention must include lawyers of a Scottish ilk, there is no rule that any Scottish law lord will sit on an appeal from the Scottish courts. As noted in Chapter 1, concerns have been voiced over the years that the current system has led, on occasion, to the erroneous imposition of English legal principles and has contributed to the demise of Scots law. The extent to which this is true is perhaps debatable; for a detailed discussion see Paterson, Bates and Poustie (1999, pp 91–94).

Any decision by the House of Lords is only given legal force when the judgment is applied in the Inner House of the Court of Session. Although the *quorum* of judges is three, in practice it is usual for a panel of five judges to hear any appeal.

It should be noted that, at the time of writing, in an effort to provide a more representative higher-tier judiciary and separate the functions of the judiciary from the influence of the executive, the Constitutional Reform Act 2005 has recently been enacted. Coming into force in October 2009, the new Act will create a new Supreme Court of the United Kingdom which will replace the House of Lords as a final court of appeal (many functions of the Privy Council will also be assimilated within the new court). The Act will thus put an end to the current judicial role of the Lord Chancellor and Law Lords.

European Court of Justice

As noted in Chapter 2, the purpose of the European Court of Justice ("ECJ") is to ensure compliance with the European Treaties and secondary legislation enacted thereunder across Member States. The ECJ is based in Luxembourg and comprises some 27 judges and eight independent court advisers known as advocates-general. The advocates-general, who have no counterpart in the domestic courts of Scotland, are a reflection of the inquisitorial nature of the ECJ procedures. Advocates-general are court officials who provide advice to the judges in the form of a detailed opinion on the legal issues at hand. Both judges and advocates-general are appointed for a 6-year period. The court generally sits "in plenary" which means that all the judges of the court hear the case. Less difficult cases, however, may be decided in chambers in front of three, five or seven judges. The court also encompasses a Grand Chamber, comprising 11 judges which sits whenever requested by a Member State or EC institution that is party to proceedings.

The domestic Scottish courts are able to refer a point of EC law central to deliberations in their current case to the European Court of Justice (ECJ). Moreover, any court or tribunal from which there is no right of appeal in Scotland is bound to refer any interpretation of a point of EC law to the ECJ. Any judgments of the ECJ only become legally enforceable by their implementation in the domestic courts of the Member State concerned. In addition to dealing with referrals from the domestic courts of Member States, the ECJ has jurisdiction in a number of other EC matters including taking action against Member States that are in violation of EC law and the judicial review of the acts of the institutions of the EU.

A Court of First Instance (CFI) was also established by virtue of the Single European Act 1986 (an EC Treaty) to help alleviate the caseload of the ECJ. The CFI handles various cases including those relating to competition law and judicial review. The CFI has been substantially reformed in the recent aftermath of the enlargement of the EU. For example, there are now "judicial panels" that can hear appropriate cases on a preliminary basis with a right of appeal to the CFI.

Civil court remedies

There are a number of remedies that civil courts may grant. These include the following:

- *specific implement*: an order to carry out a particular act, eg performance of a contract;
- *interdict*: an order prohibiting the commission or continuation of a particular act, eg publication of a defamatory article. An "interim interdict" is a temporary interdict ordered pending a full court hearing dealing with the matter complained of;
- *damages*: an order that one party pay financial compensation to the other commensurate with any loss or injury sustained;
- *declarator*: a declaration that a party has a specific right or duty;
- *reduction*: an order that the terms of an invalid document (such as a will) are set aside;
- *aliment*: an order to provide financial support to a spouse, eg in a divorce action.

There are a number of other particular remedies that might apply in particular cases, eg the legal separation or divorce of married couples.

Diligence and the civil courts

To aid in the enforcement of court decrees for financial compensation and the payments of debts due to creditors, different types of "diligence" may be employed which may entail the "freezing" of the debtor's property and often, ultimately, the sale of the same to make good a debt due. This section represents a mere snap-shot of the main diligence procedures.

Creditors may have recourse to a number of different diligence procedures. The most widely used processes are arrestment, attachment, diligence against earnings, and inhibition. Other forms, rarely encountered in practice, include civil imprisonment and the landlord's hypothec. A number of recent amendments to the law in this area have been made, primarily by the Bankruptcy and Diligence etc (Scotland) Act 2007. At the time of writing, further reforms are set to be implemented, such as a new "attachment of land" process.

Arrestment

Arrestment is a process by which a creditor "attaches" or freezes assets which belong to his debtor but which are currently in the possession of a third party – such as a car in a garage or shares in a company – with the effect that neither the third party nor the debtor is thereafter permitted to dispose of them. After arrestment the assets must remain in the hands of the third party. The assets merely remain frozen at this time and, while this may inconvenience the debtor, it will be of little comfort to the creditor. Subsequently, if the debtor then fails to instruct the third party to pass the assets on to the creditor, the creditor has the right to raise an action of "furthcoming", in which the assets will either pass directly to the creditor or be sold at auction and the proceeds used to pay off the debt (see *Lord Advocate* v *Royal Bank of Scotland* (1977)).

Types of arrestment. What is termed "arrestment on the dependence" (or "in security") is a type of diligence which may be employed by a creditor prior to a court decree being granted against him. It is normally available only in respect of a current debt as opposed to future debts, although it may be applied in respect of the latter where the debtor is deemed to be on the verge of insolvency (*vergens ad inopiam*) or may be considering absconding (*in meditatione fugae*) – see *Gillanders* v *Gillanders* (1966). Recent law reform has introduced the need for a court hearing to determine the need for arrestment on the dependence and the court may limit the assets against which arrestment will apply.

"Arrestment in execution" is more common. The right to resort to this kind of arrestment arises automatically after a court decree or where a contract, lease or bond states that the document in question, which is the basis of the debt, is to be registered in the Books of Council and Session or sheriff court books for preservation and execution.

Items exempt from arrestment. The debtor's earnings were formerly arrestable but are now subject to separate diligence procedures (discussed below). Certain items are not subject to arrestment, such as items which are alimentary in nature (eg to feed and clothe children: see *Cuthbert* v *Cuthbert's Trs* (1908)), items essential to the debtor's trade or profession and items deemed necessary for the well-being of the debtor and his family.

Diligence against earnings

A relatively new form of diligence, known as "diligence against earnings", was introduced by the Debtors (Scotland) Act 1987. In this context, the term "earnings" is interpreted liberally, thus including the normal wages or salary of the debtor as well as any fees, bonuses, commissions, pensions and annuities for previous services, statutory sick pay and compensation for loss of earnings. Diligence against earnings will generally follow a court decree. The right to resort to diligence against earnings will in general arise only where the debtor has first been served with a charge to pay the debt within 14 days. If the debt is not paid within the 14-day window, a "schedule of arrestment" is served on the employer by sheriff officers (if the relevant court is the sheriff court), or "messengers-at-arms" (for Court of Session debts). This schedule places an obligation upon the employer to pay a set proportion of the debtor's wages to the creditor, which will normally continue until the debt is met or the debtor leaves the service of the employer.

Attachment

Attachment is form of diligence exercised over items in the possession of the debtor. The current attachment procedures were enacted by the Debt Arrangement and Attachment (Scotland) Act 2002 to replace the recently abolished "poinding" regime. Poinding was a controversial form of diligence against goods in the possession of debtors, which received mass public opprobrium on the basis that it was an unfair, draconian measure, redolent of a bygone era of oppression against the poor.

Critics of attachment may point out that it is simply poinding under a different name. There are, however, some key differences. Attachment is applicable only in execution – ie in general after a court decree. Moreover, the procedures for attachment differ depending on whether the items to be attached are kept in the dwelling house of the debtor or kept somewhere else. The fundamental operating principle is that only in rare instances will items kept in the dwelling house (or other home) of the debtor be subject to attachment procedures.

Articles kept outwith the home. In respect of items not kept in the home, such as office premises, the process begins by the valuation of such goods by sheriff officers. At this time, particular items may be bought back ("redeemed") by the debtor at the value attributed to it by sheriff officers. After initial attachment has taken place, the debtor may not take away, sell or damage the items. If payment is not forthcoming for the goods, the items will be removed from the premises and moved to a designated location where an auction will occur. The proceeds of the auction (save an amount held back to cover the sheriff officer's expenses) will then be paid over to the creditor up to the amount of his debt, with any surplus being paid to the debtor.

Attachment of goods in the debtor's dwelling house. A sheriff may in exceptional circumstances allow attachment of goods from the debtor's home by way of an "exceptional attachment order". Again this is only possible where a court decree (or equivalent) is the basis for the debt and after a charge for payment has been made. This form of diligence is very much one of last resort. In determining whether to allow the attachment to proceed, the court must take into account a number of factors, including:

whether money advice has been given to the debtor; whether any previous "time to pay" arrangements have been arrived at; the nature of the debt; the debtor's assets, financial and family circumstances; whether any negotiated settlement has been attempted; and whether any other form of diligence might be appropriate. If an order is granted then only non-essential items may be attached by sheriff officers and, additionally, items of a sentimental nature are generally exempt. Rules similar to those applying in relation to goods outwith the dwelling home arise in respect of the debtor's buying back of goods and arrangements for auctions.

Interim attachment. This is a new diligence which, as an interim measure, serves to protect the interests of creditors considering using attachment procedure. A full attachment order would be required in due course, to dispose of the items subject to the attachment order.

Attachment of money. This new form of diligence allows the creditor to take action against money as banking instruments in the possession of the debtor.

Inhibitions

Inhibition is a type of diligence that can be employed in respect of heritable property such as land and buildings. Broadly speaking, inhibition prohibits the debtor from selling the property, or using that property in a manner which contravenes the purpose of the inhibition (eg the granting of a security right over the property).

In a similar fashion to arrestment and attachment, an inhibition is normally obtained following a court decree. It should be noted, however, that in *Karl Construction* v *Palisade* (2002), Lord Drummond Young held that an inhibition on the dependence (ie prior to a court decree or equivalent) may be incompatible with Article 1 of the First Protocol of the ECHR (the right to peaceful enjoyment of possessions). Additionally, in *Advocate General for Scotland* v *Taylor* (2003) it was held that the availability of inhibition on the dependence may not be compatible with Convention rights. This is an example of the horizontal effect of the Human Rights Act 1998, alluded to in Chapter 2. In common with arrestments, an inhibition on the dependence now requires a court hearing to saction it.

Unlike arrestment and attachment, inhibition is purely a negative remedy which ties up the property and cannot be followed by some other action which seeks to effect the sale of the property to make good the debt or transfer the property to the creditor.

Civil imprisonment

Civil imprisonment is a form of diligence which attaches to the person of the debtor rather than his assets. Imprisonment for non-payment is, rightly, extremely limited in modern society and is generally limited to situations in which the debtor is held in contempt of court or where the debt is of an alimentary nature (ie for the upkeep of a spouse or children) and the debtor wilfully refuses to pay when in fact he has the sums to do so.

THE CRIMINAL COURTS

Criminal jurisdiction

There are three courts that hold jurisdiction in Scottish criminal proceedings:

- the district court
- the sheriff court
- the High Court of Justiciary.

District court

At the base of the criminal court hierarchy is the district court. Established by virtue of the District Courts (Scotland) Act 1975, which merged different minor criminal courts in Scotland (the justice of the peace courts, burgh courts and the police courts) that hitherto had existed, district courts handle the least serious crimes, including such activities as being drunk and incapable, road traffic offences, minor shoplifting and breach of the peace. A district court will hear cases in which the alleged offence took place within its district.

District courts are generally presided over by lay judges known as "justices of the peace" (JPs). Being a JP is an honorary position, generally held by someone who could be considered as a pillar of the community. JPs receive training before being given the task to try their peers for minor criminal offences. There are no juries in the district courts, so both fact and law are determined by the JP. In view of his limited legal knowledge, the JP is given in-court guidance on points of law by a legally qualified "clerk of court". The relatively low gravity of offences tried before the court is reflected in the limited sentencing power of the JP – 60 days' imprisonment or a fine of £2,500.

In Glasgow the district courts are presided over by legally qualified judges appointed by the local authority, known as "stipendiary magistrates". These magistrates are vested with the sentencing power of a sheriff in summary proceedings: ie a maximum fine of £10,000 and 12 months' imprisonment.

The office of the JP is not without controversy. It has been contended that JPs tend to be drawn from a particular socio-demographic background (ie white, middle-class, conservative) which renders them non-representative of the public that they serve (and perhaps this is a concern that might be voiced regarding the judiciary in general). Moreover, the way in which they are appointed has led to concerns regarding their compatibility with human rights, particularly under Art 6 of the ECHR (right to a fair trial) (see R White, "Article 6, *Starrs* v *Ruxton*, *Clancy* v *Caird*, and Justices of the Peace" 2001 SLT (News) 105). New justice of the peace courts have been created by the Criminal Proceedings etc (Reform) (Scotland) Act 2007. They are currently replacing district courts on a phased basis.

The sheriff court

In this sense we are referring to the same sheriff courts and sheriffs that handle civil cases. The sheriff court hears cases which pertain to crimes more serious than those heard in the district court. There are two distinct court procedures which may be adopted. In less serious crimes, the summary procedure will apply (readers should not confuse this term with summary cause procedure in civil cases). In summary procedure, a sheriff will hear the case alone and must determine points of law relative to the case and make a judgment based on the facts proved in court. The penalties that a sheriff sitting in summary proceedings may impose are a maximum fine of £10,000 and up to 12 months' imprisonment.

In respect of more serious offences, solemn procedure will be appropriate. Here the legal issues are determined by a sheriff but the facts of the case are determined by a jury of 15 members of the public. Reflecting the higher gravity of offences alleged, under solemn procedure, the sheriff may impose an unlimited fine and a term of imprisonment of up to 5 years. In cases in which it is felt that the above sanctions would not represent an adequate punishment the sheriff may remit the case to the High Court of Justiciary, which may issue a harsher penalty.

High Court of Justiciary

Developed from the old judicial office of Justiciar, the High Court of Justiciary was established in 1672 and is the supreme criminal court in Scotland. It is truly the supreme court in that, unlike its civil counterpart, the Court of Session, its decisions cannot be appealed to the Judicial Committee of the House of Lords (established in *Mackintosh* v *Lord Advocate* (1876)).

Although traditionally the High Court was based in Edinburgh, it now travels "on circuit" to cities throughout Scotland as required, albeit with a permanent sitting in Edinburgh and Glasgow. The same judges sit in the

High Court as preside over the Court of Session. The Court consists of the Lord President (termed "Lord Justice-General" when acting in this capacity), the Lord Justice-Clerk, and all the other Court of Session judges (called "Lords Commissioners of Justiciary" in this context).

The most serious crimes in society are tried in the High Court of Justiciary, including murder, culpable homicide, serious sexual offences, armed robbery and drug trafficking. Reflecting the extreme gravity of the offences which are tried before the court, High Court judges hold an unlimited sentencing power, except that in some circumstances sentences are imposed by Parliament (eg life imprisonment for a murder conviction). A single judge presides over criminal trials to determine legal issues, with a jury of 15 responsible for deciding upon the facts of the case. Occasionally, benches of three judges preside over particularly important or complex cases.

Appeals in the High Court of Justiciary. The High Court of Justiciary is also an appeal court, with cases referred to it by its own trials and also from the sheriff court and (very rarely) district courts. Appeals are heard in the High Court Buildings in Edinburgh by a panel of three judges, although in cases of high societal import a panel of five or more judges may sit. A notable recent case heard by a full bench involved a re-casting of rape laws in Scotland (*Lord Advocate's Reference (No. 1 of 2001)* (2002)).

There are two principal categories of appeal: summary appeals and solemn appeals. Summary appeals (by way of the "justiciary roll") are generally brought by the "stated case" procedure. An appeal may be brought by the defence against conviction, sentence or both. The appellant may, further, bring fresh evidence but, generally, all appeals are made on a point of law. The prosecutor in summary procedure may appeal but only on a legal point which has led to an acquittal. Moreover, if some procedural irregularity is being alleged, either party may bring an appeal on such grounds, by virtue of "bill of suspension" (by the accused) or "bill of advocation" (by the prosecutor). In an appeal, the court may order a retrial or an acquittal; confirm the original verdict; or reduce or increase the sentence (if the appeal related to sentence).

With solemn appeals (on the "criminal appeal roll") the accused may appeal against sentence and/or conviction. The rights of appeal as to irregularity in court procedure, as arise in respect of summary appeals, may also be exercised by prosecutor and defence. The defence may again appeal on the facts only if fresh evidence is brought to the court. The prosecutor may appeal against the sentence if he is of the opinion that a harsher sentence better fits the crime. The Lord Advocate may also raise an appeal on a point of law if the accused has been acquitted. Whatever the outcome of this appeal, however, the acquittal of the accused will not be overturned.

Under s 25 of the Crime and Punishment (Scotland) Act 1997, the Scottish Criminal Cases Review Commission, an independent body comprising members of the legal profession and other relevantly qualified individuals, may remit a case to the High Court for review if it is felt that it is in the interests of justice. This power may be exercised regardless of the result of any appeals that have already been held. Examples of the Commission's work can be found at www.sccrc.org.uk.

Appeals to the Judicial Committee of the Privy Council. As noted above, the functions of the Privy Council are to be transferred to the newly created Supreme Court. Currently, however, there is a further right of appeal in Scottish criminal matters to the Privy Council. Appeal is by way of "devolution minute" only. This right relates to situations (amongst others) in which it is contended that the Scottish courts have gone beyond the powers delegated to them by the Westminster Parliament under the Scotland Act 1998. In *HM Advocate* v *H* (2002), the accused lodged a devolution minute following an amendment of the definition of rape which occurred in a decision of the High Court of Justiciary in *Lord Advocate's Reference (No 1) of 2001* (2002). He argued that, in formulating a new law, the court had breached the concept of separation of power and violated human rights considerations. Lord McLean held, however, that the High Court had merely corrected the law and the appeal was hence unsuccessful.

Criminal procedure

Any detailed exposition of criminal court procedure is outwith the scope of this book, but the following short discussion notes some of the main procedural aspects.

Criminal investigation

While the police carry out investigations into the commission of crime in Scotland, decisions regarding prosecution are taken by the Procurator Fiscal (PF), who acts on reports tendered by the police. The PF is the local representative of the Lord Advocate (Head of Crown Office and Procurator Fiscal service, currently Elish Angiolini). Given the gravity of the alleged offence at hand, a decision will be taken by the PF as to which court the case will be tried in (and, if in the sheriff court, whether the procedure should be summary or solemn). The PF may alternatively decide that it is not in the public interest for a prosecution to proceed. It should be noted that prosecution is almost always brought by the state through the PF. Private prosecution is extremely rare in Scotland.

Procedure in solemn cases

The court process begins life with a petition at the instance of the PF. The accused may be arrested on the basis of a warrant in the petition, although he may already have been arrested prior to the petition being served. The first appearance of the accused in the court process is always before a sheriff even if the case is ultimately to be determined before the High Court of Justiciary. This first hearing is termed a "first examination" and takes place in private. Nothing of any real substance occurs at this first hearing, and the accused will generally not enter any plea or declaration at this time. The PF will move for "committal" either for trial or for further examination. The accused will be kept in custody at this point unless bail is granted (see below)

At this stage the case preparation by the prosecution and defence will begin in earnest. For example, all police statements and any declaration by the accused are sent to the Crown Office and all witnesses will be interviewed ("precognosced") by the PF. The Crown Office will then determine what charges the accused will face in court (which may in fact differ from those originally set out on the petition). The accused is then served with a document known as an "indictment" that details the offences alleged, the time and place of the crime, a list of witnesses and a list of "productions" (documents to be used in evidence). The indictment will also set a date for trial.

Where the case is to be heard in the sheriff court there will be a "first diet" prior to the trial. This diet is to ensure that the parties are sufficiently prepared to proceed to trial. Where the case is to proceed to the High Court of Justiciary, previously there was no provision for a first diet as such but instead a "preliminary diet" could be held if either party gave written notice to the court requesting such a hearing. A mandatory preliminary hearing was introduced, however, by the Criminal Procedure (Amendment) (Scotland) Act 2004. The preliminary hearing, as well as a first diet in the sheriff court, may be used to deal with a number of preliminary issues prior to trial, such as a plea to the competency of the court to deal with the offence or the relevance of the charge (ie that the allegations made do not amount to an offence under Scots law). A "plea in bar of trial" may also be made at this stage, which may relate to the lodging by the defence of one of four special defences: insanity; alibi; incrimination (the blaming of another named party); or self-defence.

In both the sheriff court and the High Court of Justiciary, the next stage of the procedure is the trial. There are strict time limits within which a case must be brought to trial when an accused is in custody. It is a well-established rule that an accused in custody must be served with an indictment within 80 days. A further rule prescribed that the trial had to take place within 110 days of the accused being taken into custody. Where these time limits were not adhered to, accused persons had to be set free and were immune to further prosecution. These consequences were seen as a way to ensure fair treatment of accused persons; in particular, that the state was not empowered to lock up individuals for lengthy periods of time without bringing them forward for trial. Much to the disquiet of libertarians, however, in the aftermath of reforms enacted by the Criminal Procedure (Amendment) (Scotland) Act 2004, the situation has been altered quite radically. The 80-day rule still stands, but now the Crown has 140 days to bring an accused in custody to trial. More importantly, where the limits are not adhered to, the accused is liable to be given bail, but the charges may still be taken forward and he may be brought to trial at a later date. Where the accused is not in custody while awaiting trial, the preliminary hearing must take place within 11 months of the first examination.

Procedure in summary cases

In summary cases, the prosecution will normally commence by means of a document termed a "complaint", which details the alleged offence, the name and address of the accused and the court that the accused must attend at a given date and time. The accused will normally appear at a "first hearing", during which he will be asked to tender a plea of "guilty" or "not guilty". If the accused pleads "guilty" at this stage, sentence may be issued there and then. In respect of minor crime, which would not generally be punishable by a prison sentence, the accused may plead guilty by a letter.

Where the accused tenders a "not guilty" plea at the first hearing, the case will proceed to an "intermediate diet", during which the accused will be asked if he wishes to continue with this plea. This diet is also to confirm that both sides are ready to proceed to trial. If the plea is changed at this point to one of "guilt", then sentence may be passed immediately, although the court has the option of deferring sentence for social background reports. After the intermediate diet, the case will proceed to trial.

Bail in criminal proceedings

As alluded to above, in both summary and solemn procedure an accused may apply for "bail" (ie to be released from custody) pending trial. By contrast to common perceptions, save for a few exceptional circumstances, there is no money to be deposited in court in return for bail. A court, however, may impose a number of conditions, including that the accused will appear at the designated time at every subsequent court hearing, that he will not commit any offence on bail, that he will not interfere with any witnesses or in any other way attempt to pervert the course of justice, and that he will make himself available for identification parades or any samples to be taken from him.

The granting of bail is often a controversial issue. While a libertarian point of view leans in favour of bail on the basis that accused persons are innocent until the charges against them are proven in court, a more prevalent viewpoint in society holds that those accused of at least serious crimes should be locked up prior to trial, on the ground of public safety. The starting point, in any case, is that bail should be granted. Bail is, of course, not always forthcoming and the court may take into account a number of factors in arriving at its decision, including: where it is suspected that the accused may commit a further crime; where it is considered that the accused may abscond; where there is deemed to be a risk of interference with the course of justice; and to prevent public disorder. Appeals against a bail decision may be made by both the prosecution and defence.

Sanctions in the criminal courts

The traditional sanctions that can be imposed against offenders are fines and imprisonment (or detention in a young offenders' institution). As a rule of thumb, sentences may be reduced accordingly, for example, where there are mitigating circumstances surrounding commission of the offence, where the offender has no previous criminal record, or where an early "guilty" plea has been tendered by the accused. Additionally, over recent years, policy-makers have taken more holistic views on the issue of sentencing offenders, which might take into account other policy aims apart from punishment, such as rehabilitation, deterrence and restitution. Alternative sentencing options include the following:

- admonition (a warning, perhaps for minor offences, or where there are mitigating circumstances, or first offenders)
- community service orders (unpaid work in the community to repay society for offending behaviours)
- probation (a good behaviour bond)
- drug treatment and testing orders (to treat the causes of offending which stem from drug dependency)
- a restriction of liberty order (this kind of order, which may be monitored by electronic tagging, seeks to take the offender out of situations in which he may be prone to offending, by prohibiting him from being in defined places at particular times)
- forfeiture orders (where property used in an offence can be taken from the offender and sold)

- compensation orders (orders which require the offender to pay compensation to his victim)
- hospital or guardianship orders (the offender is to be detained in a hospital or under the guardianship of a responsible person, where he is insane or suffers from a mental disorder).

COURTS OF SPECIAL JURISDICTION

A range of other courts in Scotland hold jurisdiction in certain specified situations. Some of the more important courts are outlined below:

Scottish Land Court

The Scottish Land Court holds jurisdiction to resolve a range of farming disputes, including cases involving landlord and tenant, agriculture and crofting matters. The court is currently headed by a Court of Session judge, Lord McGhie, and three lay members with expertise in farming and crofting matters. Although the court is based in Edinburgh, it hears cases throughout Scotland.

Lands Valuation Appeal Court

This court hears appeals from decisions of local valuation appeal com-mittees. Appeals are heard by stated case on a point of law only and are generally presided over by a Court of Session judge sitting alone.

Church courts

The Church of Scotland operates a range of courts including the Kirk Session, Presbytery, Synod and General Assembly. Given the Church of Scotland's denominational status within Scotland, its courts, which deal exclusively with membership issues, sit independently from the Scottish courts with no right of appeal to the Court of Session (see *Logan* v *Presbytery of Dumbarton* (1995)). The courts of all other church denominations in Scotland do not have such independence.

Courts martial

Established within the armed forces to handle internal military disciplinary issues, these are courts of UK-wide jurisdiction. A Courts Martial Appeal Court consisting generally of three or five judges from the High Court of Justiciary may hear appeals from the courts martial. A further right of appeal to the Judicial Committee of the House of Lords may arise in matters of public interest.

Court of the Lord Lyon

Stemming from the 14th century, this court is presided over by the Lord Lyon King of Arms and exercises jurisdiction over such issues as heraldry, coats of arms and the use of clan badges. With both criminal and civil jurisdiction it may resolve disputes, fine and imprison offending individuals and seize any items of heraldry of which use or possession is unauthorised. Court decisions may be appealed to the Inner House of the Court of Session and thereafter to the Judicial Committee of the House of Lords.

Essential Facts

- There are two principal types of Scottish court: civil courts and criminal courts.
- Civil courts with jurisdiction in Scotland include the sheriff court, the Court of Session and the Judicial Committee of the House of Lords.
- Sheriff courts are presided over by sheriffs. There are three different civil procedures: the small claim, the summary cause and the ordinary cause.
- The Court of Session is based in Edinburgh and is split into two houses: the Outer House and the Inner House.
- The Outer House has a wide jurisdiction in civil matters throughout Scotland. Cases are heard by a "Lord Ordinary" who generally sits alone.
- The Inner House is primarily an appeal court. Normally a panel of three judges hears appeals from the Outer House and the sheriff courts.
- The Judicial Committee of the House of Lords comprises the Lord Chancellor and a number of Law Lords. This UK-wide court holds jurisdiction to hear Scottish appeals in civil matters.
- The House of Lords is to be replaced by a new Supreme Court. Operating from late 2009, the Supreme Court will take over the judicial functions of the House of Lords and many aspects of the work of the Privy Council.
- The Scottish courts may refer any issue governed by European Community law to the European Court of Justice (ECJ) to issue a ruling.

- Civil court remedies include specific implement, interdict, damages and declarator.

- Diligence refers to various procedures by which creditors can recover court debts through freezing (and at times selling) the property of their debtors.

- Different diligence procedures include arrestment, attachment, diligence against earnings, and inhibition.

- The criminal courts in Scotland are the district courts, the sheriff courts and the High Court of Justiciary.

- District courts represent the bottom rung of criminal judicial hearings in Scotland. Presided over by lay judges known as justices of the peace, these courts handle the most minor offences in society. District courts are set to be replaced by justice of the peace courts in late 2009.

- Sheriff courts are next in the criminal hierarchy. One of two procedures will be employed: for less serious crime, summary procedure; for more serious crime, solemn procedure. In summary cases the sheriff sits alone; in solemn proceedings, the sheriff determines issues of law and a jury of 15 members of the public determines the facts.

- At the top of the criminal hierarchy is the High Court of Justiciary, which deals with the most serious offences such as rape, murder and treason. Cases are heard by a single judge known as a "Lord Commissioner of Justice" and a jury of 15.

- The High Court is also an appeal court. A panel of at least three judges hears appeals from decisions of High Court trials and those of the sheriff courts and the district courts.

- Appeals by devolution minute only may be heard on Scottish criminal matters in the Judicial Committee of the Privy Council.

- In summary criminal procedure, prosecution is commenced on "complaint". There will be a first hearing and an intermediate diet prior to trial.

- In solemn criminal cases, prosecution is commenced on "indictment". There will be a first examination and a preliminary hearing prior to trial.

- A number of sentences can be passed down in the criminal courts, including imprisonment, fines, admonition, community service and probation.

Essential Cases

Starrs v Ruxton (2000): temporary sheriffs abolished; control over temporary sheriffs' appointment exercised by the Lord Advocate (as head of the prosecution service) was deemed contrary to the right to a fair trial under Art 6 of ECHR.

Karl Construction v Palisade (2002): an inhibition on the dependence (ie prior to a court decree or equivalent) may be incompatible with Art 1 of First Protocol of the ECHR (the right to peaceful enjoyment of possessions).

HM Advocate v H (2002): accused appealed against High Court of Justiciary's amendment of rape definition in *Lord Advocate's Reference (No 1) of 2001* (2002) on basis court had breached concept of separation of power and human rights considerations; appeal was unsuccessful.

4 ALTERNATIVES TO THE COURT PROCESS

The current judicial system relating to both criminal proceedings and civil actions in Scotland has been subject to a barrage of criticism. For example, pursuing or defending an action through the civil courts can often in practice amount to an expensive, time-consuming, confusing, adversarial and uncertain process. The civil court process has been subject to recent reforms designed to alleviate some of these difficulties. For example, from January 1994, the rules for the conduct of civil litigation in the sheriff courts were streamlined (Act of Sederunt (Sheriff Court Ordinary Cause Rules) 1993) and the commercial action rules in the Court of Session were reformed in 2004 (Court of Session Practice Note No 6 of 2004). Case management, in which judges seek to take a more active control in the timetabling of different aspects of civil cases with a view to expediting cases in a speedier fashion through the litigation process, has also begun to be implemented. Additionally, as noted above, new judges have been added to the Court of Session to bolster judicial manpower and cut down on case backlogs.

Criminal justice reform has also been high on the public and political agenda of late. In this sense, one recent reform to help the progress of criminal cases has been the imposition of a single system of administration, which arguably should streamline and simplify the criminal justice process.

It might be contended, however, that tinkering with procedures cannot paper over all the cracks of the Scottish judicial system. In civil matters, for example, there may in fact often be better ways of resolving many civil disputes. In this sense, both the state and private bodies offer (and at times the state compels the use of) a range of alternatives to the civil court process. Moreover, in criminal matters, a range of alternative mechanisms to prosecution through the court process has been devised. While some alternatives to traditional court processes, such as children's hearings, tribunals and arbitration, are well established, others, such as mediation and "drug courts", are relatively new and unproven.

CHILDREN'S HEARING PANEL

The children's hearing panel was set up under the Social Work (Scotland) Act 1968 as a method by which children generally under the age of 16 who may be in need of compulsory measures of care could be dealt with. Hearing panels are found in every local authority throughout Scotland. In each case the panel is made up of a number of appointed lay members. In any sitting of the panel a chairman and two other members (including both male and female participants) will hear the case. The current procedures for operation of the panel came into being by way of the Local Government etc (Scotland) Act 1994 but have since been updated by the Children (Scotland) Act 1995.

In every local authority, the panel is headed up by a Principal Reporter, an official who is answerable to a public body known as the Scottish Children's Reporter Administration, which operates under the Secretary of State. The reporter is responsible for the referral of cases to the panel.

The hearing is empowered merely to dispose of the case. In this sense it decides what measures should be taken in respect of the child but cannot arrive at any findings of guilt or determine questions of law or fact. These issues must first be referred to a sheriff for determination prior to forwarding the case to the panel.

There is a right of appeal to the sheriff against a decision of the panel. A right of appeal to the sheriff principal on a point of law or procedural irregularity is also available. A subsequent right of appeal exists to the Inner House of the Court of Session.

In respect of allegations of serious criminal offences, a child may be subject to general prosecution procedures in either the sheriff court or the High Court of Justiciary rather than being dealt with by the panel. In such cases, however, the panel may still be called upon for the provision of advice to the court or to determine how the matter should be disposed of.

Despite its solid reputation, it has been argued that operation of the children's hearing panel may be contrary to the right to a fair trial enshrined in Art 6 of the ECHR. The argument here is that breach of Art 6 may be triggered in that the Principal Reporter both institutes proceedings against the child concerned and acts in an advisory fashion to the panel of lay members about how the case should be disposed of (see Norrie (2000)). The recent case of *S* v *Miller* (2001) also raised doubts about the compatibility of the children's hearing system with the ECHR. In *Miller* it was argued that, as legal aid was not available for children's hearings, this might be inconsistent with the child's right to a fair trial under Art 6 of the ECHR. To meet such concerns, legally aided advice is available from a solicitor (assuming that the client qualifies) when it is learned that a referral is being made. Legal aid is not available for the hearing itself but it may be granted for dealing with any subsequent appeal. For a summary, see http://www.slab.org.uk/about_us/research/operations/review_children_legal_aid.pdf.

TRIBUNALS

The exponential rise in state intervention that has been seen in public life over recent years has given rise to a range of new dispute areas in administrative matters. Given that it has been deemed impractical to attempt to resolve this multitude of case-types through the civil courts, a wide range of administrative tribunals has been established, the purpose of which is to facilitate the quick and inexpensive resolution of such disputes. Some well-known examples include Social Security Appeals Tribunals, National Health Service Tribunals, Education Appeal Committees and Asylum and Immigration Appeals Tribunals. Tribunals are not simply found in relation to state administrative matters; these forms of dispute resolution are now found in other areas where disputes are commonly between two private parties, including employment and agricultural matters.

Tribunal procedure

The composition and procedures of tribunals vary but in general a range of common factors can be identified. In the main, tribunals are headed by a legally qualified chairperson, assisted in hearing cases by appropriately trained lay members. Tribunals are organised on a local basis and hearings are generally held openly in public. Tribunal procedures are (at least in theory) more informal and less legalistic and time-consuming than court procedures. The procedures, in practice, may in fact mirror the court process and it is not uncommon for parties to tribunal hearings to be represented by lawyers.

Administrative tribunals were established on the recommendation of the *Franks Report* (Cmnd 218, 1957) and are principally governed by the Tribunals and Inquiries Act 1958. The rationale behind the establishment of administrative tribunals was that they would be underpinned by the principles of openness, fairness and impartiality and pay regard to notions of natural justice. To ensure that such aims are met in practice, administrative tribunals in Scotland are overseen by the Scottish Committee of the Council on Tribunals, a public body answerable to Parliament.

Decisions of administrative tribunals can be challenged in two principal ways. First, a decision may be appealed (in the same way as court decisions) either on the facts or on a point of law to either an appeal tribunal, a court or a Government Minister. In addition, the decisions of administrative tribunals may be subject to the process of judicial review through the Court of Session. In general, judicial review is applicable where it is alleged that the tribunal concerned has acted outwith its powers (*ultra vires*) or contrary to principles of natural justice. This remedy is normally available only where all other avenues of objection have been exhausted. Operation of administrative tribunals in the UK was recently reorganised by the Tribunals, Courts and Enforcement Act 2007.

Employment tribunals

A tribunal of particular importance is the employment tribunal, primarily regulated under the Employment Tribunals (Constitution and Rules of Procedure) Regulations 2004. These tribunals are able to hear an array of employment disputes including sexual, racial and disability discrimination, equal pay and unfair dismissal. Indeed, such cases must be brought to the tribunal rather than the civil court. A tribunal is chaired by a legally qualified party, normally assisted by two lay members, one drawn from each side of the trade union/employers' association divide. Tribunal panels are empowered to conduct proceedings in any manner they deem most suitable and, in practice, the process tends to be relatively informal when compared to court processes.

The Employment Appeal Tribunal (EAT) may hear appeals from the "awards" of tribunals on points of law. The EAT consists of a Court of Session judge aided by a number of other members with recognised skill and experience in the employment field. An additional right of appeal from the EAT may be brought to the Inner House of the Court of Session and again to the Judicial Committee of the House of Lords (in future, the Supreme Court). Recently, judicial concerns have been voiced concerning the potential incompatibility of various aspects of the employment tribunal regime with human rights obligations imposed under the HRA 1998 (see, for example, *PF Fort William* v *McLean* (2000) *The Times*, 11 August (failure to provide legal aid may be contrary to Art 6)) and compare with *McVicar* v *UK* (2002) (failure to provide legal aid is not an automatic breach of Art 6: it's a question of fact and circumstances).

Lands Tribunal for Scotland

Another important and active tribunal is the Lands Tribunal for Scotland. This tribunal holds strong links with the Scottish Land Court; the President of the Lands Tribunal is also chairman of the Scottish Land Court and they share the same offices. Their respective case dockets, however, are distinct. Whereas, as noted in Chapter 3, the Scottish Land Court deals principally with agricultural and landlord and tenant disputes, the Lands Tribunal has a statutory power to deal with various types of dispute involving land or property. At the request of disputing parties, the tribunal can act as an adjudicator in any land disputes. The rules in respect of tribunal applications are set out in the Lands Tribunal for Scotland Rules 2003.

OMBUDSMEN

An ombudsman (a concept imported from Scandinavia) is a public official whose function is to investigate complaints made by the public. Ombudsmen are present in both the public sector (handling complaints from members of the public who claim to have suffered "injustice" against state bodies for misconduct ("maladministration")) and in the private sector (where complaints by consumers in relation to particular industries can be investigated).

Public bodies' maladministration

Where Scottish public bodies are involved, the role of the ombudsman has changed radically in recent times. In the early post-devolution days, complaints of maladministration levied against public bodies in Scotland were made to the Scottish Parliamentary Commissioner for Administration (SPCA). The Scottish Public Services Ombudsman Act 2002, however, set up a new office of ombudsman to assume the role of the SPCA. The new Scottish Public Services Ombudsman (SPSO) also swallowed up the functions of other pre-existing officials including the Health Commissioner for Scotland, Housing Association Ombudsman for Scotland and Local Government Ombudsman. The SPSO is formally appointed by the monarch but, in practice, at the request of the Scottish Parliament.

The SPSO may hear complaints directly from members of the public and is empowered to launch investigations in this respect. In general, the SPSO is empowered to require any member or officer of the public body concerned to supply information or produce documents. The SPSO may also require the attendance of such persons for examination. Investigations may be followed by a report (or indeed a report may be written on a decision not to investigate).

Other ombudsmen

Ombudsmen have lately become a common feature of commercial life in Scotland. They can now be sought out by disaffected consumers in a number of industry sectors, including banking, insurance, estate agency, financial services and a spate of other business spheres.

ARBITRATION

Arbitration is a long-established mode of civil dispute resolution which has existed in many forms in Scotland since as early as the 13th century (see Hunter (2002)). It also represents one of the rare areas of legal policy in Scotland in which an Act of the Old Scottish Parliament, the 25th Article of Regulation 1695, has some import in the modern day.

In short, in an arbitration the disputing parties agree to appoint a private judge, termed an "arbiter", to resolve their impasse instead of resorting to civil litigation through the courts. Reflecting the desire to avoid litigation, arbitration is a binding, legally enforceable process. The arbiter's decision (or "award") is generally final and the availability of appeals against decisions to the civil courts exists only in very limited circumstances (as discussed further below).

Arbitration is, with some notable exceptions, a voluntary process in which parties choose to eschew litigation in favour of this form of private adjudication. Parties may simply agree to attempt arbitration when a dispute arises, or may have previously entered into a contract which binds them to attempt arbitration if any dispute pertaining to the contract arises. Additionally, the ACAS Arbitration Scheme (Great Britain) Order 2004 has empowered ACAS (the Advisory, Conciliation and Arbitration Service) to prepare an arbitration scheme for the resolution of disputes arising from unfair dismissal claims.

Arbitration conduct

Arbitration is a flexible process in Scotland, primarily regulated by common law principles that have been established and refined by the courts over the centuries. Nevertheless, a number of statutory provisions do have a role to play, albeit largely on the fringes of arbitral practice, such as the 25th Article of Regulation 1695, the Arbitration (Scotland) Act 1894 and the Administration of Justice (Scotland) Act 1972.

The common law basis of arbitration has resulted in a somewhat light regulatory touch which allows the conduct of arbitral proceedings to be determined by the parties to the dispute. In terms of choice of arbiter, again the disputing parties may appoint any individual whomsoever. In practice, suitably qualified persons include solicitors or advocates of some professional standing and experience or, commonly, a professional imbued with relevant expertise and skill in the area of dispute, such as an accountant, architect, surveyor or chartered engineer. In this sense, it can be argued that matters may be resolved more quickly and in a more informed fashion by those with appropriate technical skill and experience in the dispute area. In practice, arbiters tend to be drawn from lists of accredited arbiters held by professional associations such as the Chartered Institute of Arbiters (Scotland) or the British Academy of Experts. On occasion, disputing parties may be unable to reach agreement on appointment. Some commercial contracts, for example, will make provision for both parties to appoint an arbiter. If two arbiters hearing a dispute cannot reach agreement on the award then provision may be made for the appointment of a third arbiter, termed an "oversman", to reach the final decision.

Appeals in arbitration

As noted above, arbitration awards may be appealed in limited circumstances. Awards cannot be appealed on the facts. The main grounds of appeal include:

- *"Corruption, bribery or falsehood"*. These terms are found in the antiquated provisions of the 25th Article of Regulation 1695. In practice very few awards are overturned on this ground (*Morisons* v *Thomson's Trs* (1880)). Moreover, it has become clear that if an arbiter is negligent or makes an innocent error in making an award, then this will not fall within these grounds for appeal (*Adams* v *Great North of Scotland Railway* (1891)).

- *The arbiter must not have any undisclosed conflict of interest in the proceedings* (*Sellar* v *Highland Railway* (1919), although any such conflict of interest may be waived by the disputing parties (*Tancred, Arrol & Co* v *Steel Co of Scotland* (1890)).

- *The award is defective or has gone beyond the terms of its reference* (*ultra fines compromissi*). Where an award is completely unintelligible or is in a form contrary to that which the parties specified then the court may reduce it. If the award is ambiguous but open to logical interpretation, then a court may place its own interpretation on it. The award must also exhaust the terms of the submission (*Donald* v *Shiell's Executrix* (1937)). By contrast, the award must only pertain to the issues put before the arbiter for his determination. Any other issues resolved by the arbiter may be ignored by the parties.

- *Defective procedure.* Where the arbitral procedure does not conform with that prescribed by the parties or fails to be carried out in accordance with principles of natural justice, the award may be reduced on those grounds.

Arbitration in practice

Arbitration procedures have become very popular in a number of different dispute areas. The principal attraction of arbitration is that it may be a quick, cost-effective, informal and confidential alternative to litigation through the civil courts. In practice, however, particularly in respect of commercial disputes, concerns have been raised that arbitration has in many senses become litigation by another name. The increased participation of lawyers in the arbitral process has generally led to commercial arbitration becoming an increasingly legalistic, formal and hence expensive exercise. In addition, whereas in the civil courts the costs of court buildings and salaries of judges are met from the public purse, in arbitration the costs of the arbiter, any legal clerk in attendance and the venue must be met by the disputing parties.

In order to reverse some of the current deleterious trends in commercial arbitration in Scotland and perceived deficiencies in its procedure, commentators have long called for the enactment of new arbitration laws (see Davidson (1993)). To this end, at the time of writing, the Arbitration (Scotland) Bill is proceeding through the Holyrood parliamentary procedure with a view to enactment in 2009. The Bill represents a significant shift from a primarily common law regime to one based primarily upon statutory provisions.

ADJUDICATION IN CONSTRUCTION DISPUTES

Under the Housing Grants, Construction and Regeneration Act 1996, the use of adjudication is compelled in most construction contracts to resolve disputes arising therefrom. This short form of arbitration involving determination of disputes by a designated expert is thus imposed upon the parties. Moreover, any awards issued have "temporary finality", ie they are rendered binding until the contract is completed. Proponents of the regime have pointed to its benefits in representing an inexpensive, speedy process which allows for the expediting of construction contracts. On the contrary, it could be argued that adjudication in practice leads to poorly informed decisions. Moreover, the fact that awards stemming from this new procedure can be challenged after completion of the contract may mean that in practice adjudication commonly represents merely an additional step in the process of dispute resolution. It should also be noted that the compulsory nature of the procedure and tight timeframes for dispute determination may entail certain human rights concerns (see Macauley (2000)).

ALTERNATIVE DISPUTE RESOLUTION

Modern times have seen the seeking out and development of new, generally more consensual, alternative dispute resolution forms (ADR). The dominant ADR procedure is known as mediation. In mediation the parties are encouraged to reach their own solution to their impasse by means of a third party neutral or "mediator". As well as being a consensual process, the ethos behind mediation is party empowerment, unlike traditional litigation and arbitration in which decisions are imposed upon the litigants. Other perceived benefits include the speed and low costs of mediation when compared to traditional means of resolving disputes.

Although the resolution of employment disputes by the Advisory, Conciliation and Arbitration Service (ACAS) using consensual methods can be seen as the forerunner in Scotland as regards ADR, a spate of developments in ADR has since taken place in the family, commercial and neighbourhood disputes spheres, as well as in criminal matters. Outwith family and community matters, mediation practice has historically remained modest, albeit that some progress seems to have been made in more recent times. Barriers to mediation's development may include a lack of recognised standards in the regulation and training of neutrals, ignorance of, and perhaps active resistance to, mediation on the part of both lawyers and disputing parties, and the fact that mediation can never guarantee settlement.

Mediation in family disputes

The first family mediation developments took place in Scotland in the late 1980s when a pilot programme was established in the Lothian region. Since then family mediation has developed across Scotland under an umbrella organisation, "Relationships Scotland", and a group of family lawyers specialists, termed "Comprehensive Accredited Lawyer Mediators" (CALM). Mediation services may be offered in respect of disputes pertaining to custody of, and access to, children and also financial and property settlements arising from legal separation or divorce. In matrimonial matters, both the sheriff courts and the Court of Session are now empowered to refer disputing parties to mediation if it is deemed appropriate (Ordinary Cause Rules, r 33.22; Rules of the Court of Session 1994, r 49.23).

Commercial mediation

A number of private, for-profit, commercial mediation providers now operate in Scotland, including "Core Mediation" and "Catalyst Mediation".

Commercial mediation has not developed as quickly in Scotland as was hitherto expected but a recent, high-profile, in-court advice and mediation project in Edinburgh Sheriff Court may have served to increase publicity in this relatively new form of dispute resolution (see Samuel (2002)). Furthermore, the sheriff court rules were recently amended so that sheriffs may refer parties to mediation in appropriate cases (Act of Sederunt (Ordinary Cause Rules) Amendment (No 3) (Commercial Actions) 2000, r 40.12(3)(m)). A review of civil justice is currently ongoing, under the auspices of Lord Gill (Scottish Civil Courts Review: A Consultation Paper (Scottish Executive, 2007)). At the time of writing, the review has not yet been reported but it may well encourage the use of more commercial mediation in Scotland through court referral.

Mediation in community/neighbourhood disputes

Mediation programmes have become a well-known feature of community life in Scotland over recent years. A number of pilot schemes, including those in Edinburgh, Dundee, Kirkcaldy, Livingston and Glenrothes, have been established since 1995 under the aegis of charitable bodies such as Mediation UK and SACRO (Safer Communities Reducing Offending). Such programmes, typically operated by locally trained volunteer mediators, seek to assist members of the community to resolve a wide range of typical neighbourhood disputes including noise pollution, problems with the behaviour of children and pets, harassment and boundary issues. For a review of some of the early Scottish schemes, see Mackay and Brown (1998).

General

The Scottish Mediation Register, an independent body with a register of mediators in Scotland, all of whom have basic "benchmark" standards such as training and codes of conduct, has recently been established. This encompasses varous sectors, including Business and Commercial, Discrimination; and Family.

DIVERSIONS FROM PROSECUTION

Recent years have seen the development of a spate of initiatives in which those who have committed offending behaviour are dealt with in some alternative manner rather than the normal criminal court process. The aim of such "diversion from prosecution" is two-fold: first, to avoid clogging up the criminal justice system, to find more efficient ways of dealing with perpetrators of minor crime; and, second, a belief that handling certain offences in different ways may lead to superior outcomes, particularly in pursuance of the aim of reducing recidivism (re-offending) and, in some cases, meeting the needs of victims more effectively. While some might claim that these kinds of initiatives are soft options, pandering to liberal ideologies, many programmes have in practice been successful in meeting at least some of the aims highlighted above.

Fiscal fines

The Criminal Justice (Scotland) Act 1987 made provision for the "fiscal fine", whereunder, in respect of the commission of minor crimes, accused persons would simply be fined instead of being prosecuted through the district court. The powers in this regard have since been extended by the Criminal Justice (Scotland) Act 1995. Generally, if the accused person accepts an offer by the procurator fiscal to pay a fiscal fine then the prosecution does not proceed and the accused receives no criminal record.

Diversion to a voluntary organisation

This kind of diversion may occur where there is deemed to be no public interest in prosecuting an individual. The offender may be offered an opportunity to attend an appropriate voluntary organisation instead, which may, for example, deal with any drug or alcohol dependency that has fuelled the commission of crime.

Mediation as a diversion from prosecution

A number of pilot schemes have been developed throughout Scotland by SACRO that refer accused persons to mediation programmes where they attend face-to-face sessions with the victims of their crimes and provide some form of compensation to their victims instead of being prosecuted through the criminal courts. It is argued that such programmes may benefit offenders, in helping them to see the error of their ways (and hence reduce re-offending), and also be of value to victims, whose psychological and material needs may be addressed more effectively than through the court system.

Fixed penalty notices

Fixed penalties are commonplace in respect of minor road traffic offences, where payment of a set amount will result in no prosecution being brought against the driver. Many such offences also result, of course, in the endorsement of the perpetrator's driving licence.

Drug courts

Drug courts were piloted in Glasgow and Fife in 2001 and 2002. The aim of these special courts is to divert offenders, whose criminal behaviour has been fuelled by drug dependency, from an oft-continuous replay of prosecution through the courts into medical treatment programmes. It is hoped that appropriate medical treatment may deal with the root cause of the offending behaviour and thus lead to the rehabilitation of the individual concerned. Whether drug courts have been a success is debatable. In a report of March 2006, it was stated that 50 per cent of those handled by the drug court were re-convicted within 1 year and 71 per cent within 2 years (see "The Operation and Effectiveness of the Scottish Drug Court Pilots", 30 March 2006, p 4 (available at: http://www/scotland.gov.uk/Publications/2006/03/28112035/12).

FATAL ACCIDENT INQUIRIES

After the occurrence of a fatal accident in Scotland (eg in the workplace), a fatal accident inquiry will be held (the equivalent in England is a coroner's inquest). The purpose of the inquiry is to ascertain the facts surrounding the death rather than to apportion any blame as such. The inquiry is set up by the procurator fiscal and takes place in the sheriff court. In the course of the inquiry, evidence will be led, and submissions made in court by the procurator fiscal. Additionally, any interested parties such as relatives, employers or colleagues may be called upon to take part in the inquiry, and may be represented at the inquiry by lawyers. At the conclusion of evidence and submissions, the sheriff will make a determination setting out the circumstances of the death, indicating where and when the accident resulting in the death took place, along with the causes of both the accident and the death.

Essential Facts

- Tribunals are provided by the state as a means by which administrative, employment, land and other forms of dispute can be resolved without proceedings in the civil courts. Tribunals are perceived to be characterised by the benefits of flexibility, speed, informality and openness.

- Arbitration involves the resolution of disputes by a private judge known as an arbiter. Arbitration is common in commercial matters and represents a legally enforceable process in which appeals of arbitral awards are available only in very limited circumstances.

- Ombudsmen are officials who can investigate complaints made by the public in a number of areas of the public and private sector.
- The ADR process is mediation in which disputants are assisted by a mediator to resolve their dispute. Perceived benefits include speed, cheapness, informality, party empowerment and confidentiality. Mediation is common in family matters but not so in other civil dispute areas.
- Children's hearing panels are a well-established method of dealing with children under the age of 16 in need of compulsory care orders.
- There are a number of different schemes which seek to divert offenders from prosecution, including fiscal fines, drug courts and criminal mediation programmes.

Essential Cases

S v Miller (2001): legal aid being unavailable for children's hearings might be inconsistent with child's right to a fair trial under ECHR, Art 6; reforms enacted to provide for legal aid in some circumstances.

Morisons v Thomson's Trs (1880): not corrupt for an arbiter to first request a loan of £1,000 from one party in a dispute in which he was arbitrating and then request same from the other party; the arbiter knew both parties, so any undue influence was unlikely to arise in the circumstances.

Donald v Shiell's Executrix (1937): an arbitration sought determination of two issues in dispute re rights of incoming and outgoing farm tenants; failed to deal with both issues, so entire terms of award could be reduced.

5 LEGAL PERSONNEL

In this chapter we review some of the key players in the Scottish legal system, including legal professionals, legal officials of the Crown, judges and jurors.

SOLICITORS

The Scottish legal profession can be broken into two distinct streams of lawyer: solicitors and advocates. By far the most prevalent legal professional in Scotland is the solicitor. Solicitors' work may vary significantly: the wide range includes issuing legal advice to the public, drawing up legal documents, organising the affairs and distributing the estates of deceased persons, undertaking the buying and selling of land and buildings ("conveyancing") and court work. Solicitors can thus properly be viewed as "general practitioners" of the law. Solicitors may hold many different employment arrangements, including working in private practice either alone or in partnership (or working as employees for such law firms); working "in-house" for large commercial concerns; or as employees of public and local authorities.

As noted above, some solicitors represent their clients in both criminal and/or civil courts. Historically speaking, solicitors did not enjoy "rights of audience" (the right to appear on behalf of clients) in the superior courts (Court of Session, High Court of Justiciary and House of Lords). By virtue of the provisions of the Solicitors (Scotland) (Rights of Audience in the Court of Session, the House of Lords and the Judicial Committee of the Privy Council) Rules 2002, solicitors may undertake further training and qualify as a "solicitor-advocate". Designation as solicitor-advocate grants the individual extended rights of audience to appear in Scotland's superior courts.

Generally speaking, non-lawyers (other than the parties themselves) have no rights of audience in the Scottish courts. Some notable exceptions to this rule include the small claims procedure in the sheriff court and certain sheriff court proceedings under the Debtors (Scotland) Act 1987 where suitable non-lawyers may be given permission by the court to represent parties.

Regulation

The Law Society of Scotland (LSS), currently governed by the Solicitors (Scotland) Act 1980, and established in 1949, regulates the solicitors' profession. Every practising solicitor must be a member of the LSS and may only practise law if issued with a "practising certificate" by the LSS. The LSS has a number of functions, principally including: responsibility for setting appropriate admission, education and ongoing professional development standards; regulating standards of practice; and disciplining misconduct. In serious cases of misconduct, solicitors may be cited to appear before a Scottish Solicitors' Discipline Tribunal, which is empowered to issue a fine of up to £10,000, suspend or disbar the solicitor from practice in addition to ordering retraining of any staff involved in the complaint.

The LSS is a self-regulating body (ie the profession regulates itself). In addition to its regulatory functions, the LSS also promotes the interests of its members and acts as a pressure group in the political system. The extent to which these two functions can co-exist in the same body has been questioned. In response to such concerns, as of 1 October 2008, complaints regarding the service provided by legal practitioners (both solicitors and advocates) have been dealt with by a new, independent Scottish Legal Complaints Commission. As noted above, complaints regarding alleged professional misconduct of solicitors will still be dealt with by the LSS and those in respect of advocates by the Faculty of Advocates.

The LSS is also responsible for the maintenance of a Guarantee Fund, to which all solicitors must contribute. The fund may be used to meet the compensation needs of clients who have suffered financial loss at the hands of errant solicitors. In this sense, solicitors may be held personally liable in damages for their negligent acts, through civil court actions brought by disaffected clients. Solicitors are under a general delictual duty to act with due diligence and skill and hence must act in such a fashion as might reasonably be expected of skilled, legal professionals (for some examples, see *Evans* v *Stool* (1885); *Stewart* v *McLean, Baird & Neilson* (1915)).

Training

The majority of solicitors will have first gained a law degree (LLB) from a Scottish University, followed by a more practically oriented Diploma in Legal Practice (DipLP). A fledgling solicitor then undertakes a two-year "traineeship" within private practice or with a public authority, and also attends a two-week Professional Competence Course, prior to receiving their practising certificate. While in practice, solicitors are placed under a continuing obligation to bolster and update their professional skills by undertaking a number of hours of Continuing Professional Development (CPD) annually. It should be noted that, at the time of writing, the Law Society of Scotland is finalising its plans for a shaking-up of educational requirements for would-be entrants to the profession. The consultation process can be tracked at: http://www.lawscot.org.uk/training/.

Notaries public

Many solicitors are also notaries public. This is an old professional role which, since 1896, can only be assumed by solicitors. The functions of a notary public include: attesting or authenticating powers of attorney, particularly abroad; the administration of oaths; and particular activities in respect of certain commercial and maritime documents.

ADVOCATES

Advocates are far less common in number than solicitors, and at least traditionally can be said to represent the elite of the legal profession in Scotland, although some solicitors (and other commentators) might argue with that! As a reflection of this view, advocates historically held exclusive rights of representation in the superior Scottish courts. Their monopoly, however, was removed by the extension of rights of audience in such courts to solicitor-advocates.

Advocates can further be split into "junior counsel" and "senior counsel", also termed "Queen's Counsel" (QC). An advocate may be appointed to the status of QC after gaining appropriate experience and reputation. This process is known as "taking silk", so named as the advocate is entitled, on becoming a QC, to wear a silk robe in court. The profession of advocates is known collectively as "the Bar", a term derived from the bar that runs along one side of the Court of Session, behind which advocates stand in court.

Advocates are sole practitioners and, unlike solicitors, are barred by professional rules from establishing partnerships (although they may work together on a particular case). Advocates are attached to "stables", however. Stables are groupings of advocates and each stable is serviced by a clerk who takes instructions from solicitors and distributes work to the advocates. A separate service company, Faculty Services Ltd, provides administrative and secretarial support.

A quirk of the system that may perplex readers is that the client is generally not able to contract or make any contact with an advocate directly but only through the offices of a solicitor. It also generally follows that in respect of meetings between an advocate and his client, a solicitor must be present. Having said that, persons belonging to particular professional bodies may instruct advocates directly, such as architects, surveyors and engineers.

"Opinions of counsel" are often sought from advocates. In this sense we are referring to advice sought by a party through his solicitor with regard, for example, to interpretation of a particular area of law or the analysis of some contractual provision where some element of doubt exists. The advocate's opinion may often be sought by parties contemplating involvement in litigation proceedings. The advice may give such parties a more informed view of their legal position and indicate their prospects of success.

Regulation

Scottish advocates are regulated by the Faculty of Advocates. This body is headed by the Dean of the Faculty and its principal remit is to set appropriate standards for admission, qualifications and professional conduct. As noted above, service complaints made against advocates are dealt with by the Scottish Legal Complaints Commission. Regarding professional misconduct, although most disciplinary cases are handled in-house through a "complaints committee", serious cases may be remitted to a Discipline Tribunal, which is empowered to censure, issue a fine of up to £15,000, suspend or disbar an advocate from practice.

In what may seem to be a somewhat inequitable proposition, generally speaking, unlike the case with solicitors, it is a customary rule of law that advocates cannot be sued in the civil courts for negligence, albeit that a remedy would arise where the advocate had acted fraudulently (see, for example, *Swinfen* v *Lord Chelmsford* (1860)).

Training

The route to becoming an advocate, at least initially, mirrors that for solicitors. Most advocates hold a university law degree and Diploma in Legal Practice. This legal education will generally be followed by a year's work as a trainee in a legal office followed by engagement for a 9-month period as a pupil of an established advocate (this process is known as "devilling"). Perhaps redolent of the traditionally elitist nature of the advocacy profession, devilling is normally carried out for no payment, albeit that scholarships are now available.

CONVEYANCING AND EXECUTRY PRACTITIONERS AND PARALEGALS

In a move that removed a hitherto monopoly for solicitors, two new forms of legal professional – licensed conveyancers and executry practitioners – were established by the Law Reform (Miscellaneous Provisions) (Scotland) Act

1990. A Scottish Conveyancing and Executry Board was set up to regulate these new occupational roles. The provisions of the 1990 Act created something of a hullabaloo, particularly as it was felt by solicitors that the conveyancing market would become saturated and fees would drop to rock bottom levels (colloquially termed "bucket conveyancing"). Such fears have been largely unfounded, however, and these new vocational opportunities have not proven especially popular. The Conveyancing and Executry Board was abolished in 2003 by way of the Public Bodies and Public Appointments etc (Scotland) Act 2003. The Board's functions have now been transferred to the Law Society of Scotland.

Other types of often part-qualified, legal professionals, broadly termed "paralegals", frequently work in support of solicitors in many different legal spheres, particularly conveyancing, executries and criminal work.

LAW OFFICERS OF THE CROWN

The Law Officers of the Crown are the Crown's official legal advisers. The two principal officers – the Lord Advocate and the Solicitor General for Scotland – are members of the Scottish Executive and represent the Crown in Scotland (now the Scottish Executive) in both criminal and civil matters. In addition, the Lord Advocate is the head of the Crown Office and thus has ultimate responsibility for overseeing criminal prosecutions in Scotland. Advocates Depute, appointed by the Lord Advocate, appear in the bulk of High Court of Justiciary cases. On rare occasions, either the Lord Advocate or the Solicitor General will themselves appear. Procurators fiscal (and their deputes) represent the Crown in cases in the inferior criminal courts. By virtue of the Scotland Act 1998, the Lord Advocate and the Solicitor General are appointed by the Queen but in practice appointment is made on the recommendation of the First Minister and with the approval of the Scottish Parliament. A third Scottish Crown Law Officer – the Advocate General for Scotland – is a member of the UK Government. The role of the Advocate General is to offer advice to the Westminster Government on legal issues pertaining to Scotland.

THE JUDICIARY

In common with England and Wales, there is no separate professional grouping that constitutes the judiciary. The relevant qualifications for the judiciary are outlined in the discussion of the courts in Chapter 3; generally speaking, the judiciary comprises suitably experienced and skilled members of either the solicitors' or (more commonly in practice) the advocates' profession. The fact that there exists no separate profession of judges, akin, for example, to that which exists in the French legal system, can be criticised on the basis that the role of judge is fundamentally different to the role of solicitor or advocate. Nevertheless, any newly appointed members of the judiciary would have gained significant experience of the court process and the analytical legal skills developed as lawyers are clearly relevant to the judicial role. Another important policy issue regarding the judiciary pertains to the wide and varied nature of legal issues in the docket of cases that judges may be required to determine, often spanning the whole gamut of civil and criminal areas of law. This factor may raise doubts as to the ability of our custodians of justice to apply the law in a correct fashion in every case in practice. In terms of different legal spheres, the judiciary may have to be "jacks of all trades", but, to be fair, many may be legitimately described as "masters of most".

Appointments

Scotland's most senior judges – the Lord President and the Lord Justice-Clerk – are technically appointed by the Crown on the advice of the Prime Minister, who receives recommendations from the First Minister.

Other Court of Session and High Court judges and sheriffs were hitherto appointed to office by the Crown acting on the recommendation of the Secretary of State for Scotland. The Lord Advocate also played an advisory role in such judicial appointments. In light of concerns voiced regarding a lack of transparency and accountability in the incumbent system (including disquiet about the fact that the Lord Advocate may recommend his own elevation to the Bench) and potential incompatibilities with human rights obligations, a Judicial Appointments Board comprising senior judges and lay members was set up in 2001 by the Justice Minister to oversee the recruitment and appointment of judges. The Board began its functions in June 2002 and, under the new regime, Court of Session judges (who also sit in the High Court of Justiciary) remain technically appointed by the Crown, on the advice of the First Minister, following consultation with the Lord President. The role of the Judicial Appointments Board is to interview applicants through an open selection process and pass on its recommendations to the First Minister. It should also be noted that, on implementation of the Constitutional Reform Act 2005 in October 2009, an independent selection commission comprising, *inter alia*, a member of the Scottish Judicial Appointments Board and a member from its counterparts in England and Wales, and Northern Ireland will appoint members to the new Supreme Court. Temporary judges may be appointed (from time to time as the need arises) by the First Minister on the advice of the Lord President.

Generally, judges appointed prior to 31 March 1995 must retire before the age of 75. Those appointed thereafter are bound to retire at the age of 70 (subject to an eligibility to sit as "retired judges" until the age of 75).

Sheriffs are again appointed by the Crown, on the recommendation of the First Minister, who is bound to consult with the Lord President. The Judicial Appointments Board considers applications from those seeking appointment and furnishes recommendations in this sense to the First Minister. Sheriffs appointed prior to 31 March 1995 must retire at the age of 72. Those appointed thereafter are bound to retire at 70. Part-time sheriffs may be appointed by the First Minister, from time to time as the need arises.

Justices of the peace (JPs) are generally appointed by local Justice of the Peace Advisory Committees, although a minority may be appointed by local authorities in an *ex officio* capacity. Stipendiary magistrates are appointed by the Scottish Ministers on the advice of a sheriff principal.

Liability and removal of judges

Judges are historically immune from any civil action brought against them by any disaffected parties – a rule that can be traced back to the time of Stair. The principal rationale underlying this is that the courts might find themselves awash with claims for compensation from parties unhappy with one aspect or another of a court's decision.

It is possible (although extremely rare in practice) that members of the judiciary may, however, be removed from office for misconduct. In respect of judges in the Court of Session and High Court of Justiciary, they may be removed from office by the Crown on the recommendation of the First Minister following a resolution of the Scottish Parliament. In order to assuage fears that the right of Parliament to remove judges would inhibit the independence of judges and insert political expediencies into the judicial function, in order for removal to take place, prior to a parliamentary resolution to this effect, a tribunal, headed by a member of the Privy Council, must have reported that the judge concerned was unfit for office either by inability, neglect of duty or misbehaviour.

For sheriffs, a similar process applies, in which the Secretary of State for Scotland may issue an order for the removal of a sheriff from office where the Lord President and Lord Justice-Clerk have furnished him with a report recommending such removal. An order to this effect by the Secretary of State is subject to annulment by the Scottish Parliament. At the time of writing, two sheriffs have been removed from office: Sheriff Peter Thomson, in 1977, for political activities deemed incompatible with his judicial office; and Sheriff Ewen Stewart, in 1992, who was removed on the ground of inability.

JPs may be removed from office after a recommendation to this effect by a tribunal consisting of three members appointed by the Lord President.

JURORS

Members of the public, sitting as jurors, perform a pivotal role in the Scottish legal system, particularly in criminal matters. The premise behind the role of juries in criminal trials is that if a party has been accused of a criminal matter for which he ought to be punished by society then his guilt should be determined by his peers. The jury is thus seen as a cornerstone of a civilised criminal justice system. Of course, as noted in Chapter 3, juries do not sit in less serious, summary criminal trials in the sheriff and district courts, where facts are determined by the judge.

It is worth noting that the jury system has been criticised of late, particularly in respect of lengthy, technical trials. The suggestion here is that juries may very easily become bamboozled, perplexed and perhaps bored when faced with a mountain of technical factual and legal argument, which might lead to unsafe, irrational verdicts (see A Bonnington, "The stupidest in the world?" (2004) 49 JLSS 12). Reflecting such concerns, the UK Government recently moved to remove juries from Crown Court trials in England and Wales in complex fraud cases (under the Criminal Justice Act 2003, ss 43 and 44). Scotland has not followed suit.

In Scotland, the jury in a criminal trial comprises 15 members of the public, selected at random from the electoral register. Jurors must have been resident in the UK for at least the previous 5 years, be registered electors and be between the ages of 18 and 65. Certain classes of people are ineligible, including legal professionals and certain ex-offenders; others are disqualified, including those with a mental illness. The role of the jury is to determine factual matters (and hence, in criminal matters, whether the accused is guilty or not on the facts presented), with legal matters of the case being decided by the judge. Juries will commonly be given a "legal direction" by a judge, explaining how the law applies to the case at hand; and "misdirections" in this sense are common grounds for appeal. In criminal cases, a decision can be reached by a simple majority, with the proviso that, for a finding of guilt, eight jurors must have reached that decision (it should be noted that some jurors may have remained undecided). Jurors will appoint a spokesperson who will announce the verdict to the court after a decision has been reached.

On rare occasions, juries may be present in civil cases in the Court of Session, in which case 12 jurors would sit. Again, any civil jury must determine the facts of the case, whereas the law is decided by the judge.

Essential Facts

- Lawyers in Scotland comprise a number of distinct professional groups including solicitors, advocates, solicitor-advocates and licensed conveyancing and executry practitioners.

- Solicitors may be viewed as "general practitioners" of the law. They fulfil a number of legal roles and may represent clients in the lower courts.
- Advocates are specialist lawyers who hold rights of audience in the superior Scottish courts and commonly issue opinions (known as "counsel's opinion") on particular points of legal interpretation.
- There are various Law Officers of the Crown including the Lord Advocate, Solicitor General and Advocate General.
- Juries are composed of 15 members of the public (12 in civil cases), who determine the facts of a case generally by majority decision.
- There is no separate professional grouping of judges in Scotland. Judges are drawn from the ranks of suitably experienced advocates and solicitors.
- Judges in the superior courts and sheriffs are generally appointed by the Crown, on the advice of the First Minister, who is in turn advised by a Judicial Appointments Board.

6 LEGAL ASSISTANCE FOR THE PUBLIC

Different forms of financial and expert legal assistance are available for members of the public. Some, such as legal aid, are well established, while others, such as university law clinics, are relatively new ways in which legal assistance has been provided in recent times to meet high levels of public demand.

LEGAL AID

Legal aid relates to financial assistance made available by the state, to parties who cannot afford to pay for their own legal representation, to engage lawyers either to represent them in criminal or civil courts or to tender legal advice. Perhaps surprisingly, legal aid for the poor has existed in one form or another since as early a date as 1424. The modern law of legal aid, however, originated in the aftermath of the Legal Aid and Solicitors (Scotland) Act 1949. The current legal aid scheme is governed by the Legal Aid (Scotland) Act 1986 (as amended), and is run under the auspices of the Scottish Legal Aid Board (SLAB). The board is headed by a chairman and comprises between 11 and 15 members appointed by the First Minister; two of these must be advocates, two solicitors, one other with experience of the court system and the remainder lay members. There are two main functions of SLAB: first, to ensure that legal aid is available in accordance with statutory provisions; second, to administer the legal aid fund – a block of money (primarily made up of government grants) from which legal aid fees are paid to legal professionals.

There are in fact various, distinct species of legal aid available to parties in different circumstances, namely: legal advice and assistance; criminal legal aid; and civil legal aid.

Advice and assistance

This state financial assistance pertains to situations where a member of the public is seeking advice and assistance that falls short of representation in court (except for "Assistance by Way of Representation" (ABWOR); see below). In general, legal advice and assistance relates to oral or written advice tendered by a solicitor or advocate either on the application of law to any particular circumstances which have arisen in relation to which the party is seeking advice or as to what legal steps a party might appropriately take, such as the raising of an action in the civil court (or in fact advice as to whether such advice set out above is required). There are strict financial criteria for determining the eligibility of a party for advice and assistance. In general, a party will only be eligible for state aid in respect of their legal advice and assistance costs where their "disposable income" and "disposable capital" fall below defined statutory levels. Moreover, a sliding scale operates and, in many cases, a contribution towards the fees may be payable by the party receiving the advice. For current eligibility limits, see http://www.slab.org.uk.

The right to financial assistance for legal representation in court under ABWOR arises where a party not in custody seeks to tender a plea of "guilty" in court (or change their plea to "guilty") and no application for legal aid has yet been made.

Criminal legal aid

Criminal legal aid is available in respect of appearance in all Scotland's criminal courts. If an accused person is in custody then he may avail himself of the services of a "duty solicitor", who will be available at that time. There is no need for any formal application to be made for legal aid to make use of the duty solicitor (provided on a rota by local solicitors) and there will be no enquiry made into the accused person's financial circumstances at this time.

Any accused seeking legal aid for a criminal trial must make a formal application, either to SLAB (in summary cases) or to the court (in solemn cases). Again, the financial status of the accused will be a key factor in determining whether the legal aid will be granted. Additionally, however, either SLAB or the court may ask a number of other questions to ascertain eligibility, including:

(1) Are there any other bodies that might be obliged to meet the legal bill (such as a trade union)?

(2) Is it in the "interests of justice" that legal aid be granted? This question can further be broken down into a number of further questions, including:

(a) Might the finding of guilt lead to loss of liberty or livelihood?

(b) Is the evidence complex or legal issues substantial?

(c) Does the defence appear to be frivolous?

(d) Is it in the interests of some other person (eg the victim) that the accused be represented?

Criminal legal aid has been shrouded in controversy over recent years. In what can perhaps be considered a "golden age" for criminal legal aid practitioners, in the 1980s and early 1990s legal aid was often a lucrative business as lawyers could charge fees which varied according to the extent of work carried out on each element of their case preparation, travel costs and time spent in court. Escalating fee levels and reported sharp practice by legal professionals (including touting for clients, habitual tendering of "not-guilty" pleas to maximise revenue before a last-minute shift to an admission of guilt; and excessive, unnecessary case-preparation) eventually led, in 1999, to the introduction of "fixed fees". Fixed fees are set amounts that are paid in all summary criminal cases: £500 in a sheriff court case; and £300 in a district court case. While fixed fees can be criticised in that they give lawyers a disincentive to prepare a client's case properly and may hence lead to a two-tier system of justice, which is prejudicial to those who cannot afford to pay for their own lawyers, the new arrangements seem a reasonable public response in the face of the hitherto oft-extravagant sums that criminal legal aid lawyers were drawing from the public purse. For a recent discussion, see C Tata *et al*, "Impact of the Introduction of Fixed Payments into Summary Criminal Legal Aid: Repoort of an Independent Study" (2007) at p v (available at http://www.scotland.gov.uk/Resource/Doc/180464/005/284. pdf).

Civil legal aid

Civil legal aid is available for representation in Scotland's civil courts, a number of courts of special jurisdiction and some tribunals. This type of financial assistance is available in respect of most kinds of civil action, with some notable exceptions, including: small claims in the sheriff court (unless the action relates to personal injury); and certain bankruptcy and diligence proceedings.

Again, in terms of eligibility, the recipient must be financially eligible, the legal action or defence must not be considered spurious, and there should be no other appropriate body that is obliged to meet the bill. At the time of writing, the Scottish Government has recently signalled its intention to raise the legal aid thresholds with a view to increasing accessibility to civil justice in Scotland: see http://www.slab.org.uk/getting_legal help/ Extended_eligibility.html.

PUBLIC DEFENCE SOLICITORS' OFFICE (PDSO)

The PDSO was set up as a pilot project in 1998 for 5 years in Edinburgh under the Crime and Punishment (Scotland) Act 1997. The PDSO is a public body that provides lawyers to represent parties in summary criminal matters. Unlike the legal professionals engaged under legal aid, who are private practitioners, public defenders are civil servants employed by SLAB. Public defender programmes have attracted negative publicity, particularly in the USA, where poor levels of funding, low morale of staff and inadequate services are commonly reported. Moreover, their lack of independence from the state (the prosecuting authority) has been flagged up as a practical problem in that this may lead to the distrust of accused individuals (for an interesting review of US PDSO schemes, see B Boruchowitz, "Lessons from the United States' Public Defenders Experience", available at http://faculty.law.ubc.ca/ilac/Papers/02%20Boruchowitz.html). Initial research on the PDSO in Edinburgh was, nevertheless, at least partially favourable (in terms of, for example, the potential for costs savings, and the speedier expediting of cases through the court process – see T Goriely *et al* (2001)). In light of these findings, PDSOs have been rolled out in Glasgow, Inverness, Ayr, Dundee, Falkirk and Kirkwall. For more information about the workings of PDSOs, see http://www.slab.org.uk/pdso. Whether, in time, PDSOs will ultimately replace the provision of legal aid by the engagement of lawyers in private practice remains to be seen.

LAW CENTRES

Law centres are generally non-profit-making concerns, manned by solicitors and paralegals, that seek to fulfil unmet legal requirements in their particular locality. Law centres tend to focus on the spheres of law where there is the greatest local need, including consumer disputes, immigration issues, housing problems, employment, criminal injuries compensation, and money and debt. These services are usually offered on a "*pro bono*" (free) basis to clients. Law centres are now a common feature of community life in Scotland, particularly in heavily populated, urban areas.

CITIZENS' ADVICE BUREAUX

Citizens' Advice Bureaux (CABx) are local charitable organisations that provide advice and information to members of the public. CABx aim to ensure that individuals do not suffer legally or financially due to a lack of knowledge of, or information about, their rights and responsibilities or services available to them, or an inability to express themselves effectively. Much of the work of CABx in practice involves tendering free, confidential advice on such matters as money problems and debt control, consumer disputes, benefit entitlement, employment matters and immigration issues. On occasion, CAB advisers may represent individuals in the small claims court. CABx play a valuable role in society; they are now commonplace throughout Scotland, with over 200 offices scattered across the nation.

A recent CAB development has been the inception of "in-court" advisers. These advisers are CAB personnel who provide free, in-court support on issues such as small claims, heritable matters, rent arrears and evictions, consumer complaints, debt negotiation and benefits. Advisers can provide emergency in-court advice and guidance to those who do not have someone to represent them. These services are currently available on a pilot basis in six sheriff courts in Scotland: Aberdeen; Airdrie; Hamilton; Dundee; Edinburgh and Kilmarnock.

UNIVERSITY LAW CLINICS

At the time of writing, there is only one university law clinic in Scotland, at the University of Strathclyde in Glasgow. Such legal advice centres are commonplace in other jurisdictions, however. Law clinics are generally run by university law students under the guiding hand of law staff and external, professionally qualified legal advisers; and offer a free legal advice service to members of the public. The Strathclyde clinic offers advice on a wide range of legal areas, which typically, in practice, focus on consumer complaints, small claims (including representation in court), employment matters, benefit entitlement claims, and housing and neighbourhood disputes. For further information about services offered by the Strathclyde law clinic, see http://www.lawclinic.org.uk.

Essential Facts

- Legal aid is state-provided financial assistance for the engagement of lawyers in private practice for those who cannot afford to pay the legal costs themselves.

- Legal aid is available for legal representation in both the criminal and civil courts and also advice and assistance on interpretation of the law or any procedural steps that might be taken in respect of a legal issue.

- The Public Defence Solicitors' Office provides state-employed lawyers who may represent parties in criminal courts and provide legal advice and assistance.

- Citizens' Advice Bureaux are voluntary organisations that provide free legal advice and assistance on a range of legal issues to members of the public within their vicinity. A new "in-house" adviser scheme can provide on-the-spot advice in court.

- Law clinics are staffed by solicitors and support staff and tender legal advice on a range of legal issues to the public free of charge.
- University law clinics are legal advice and assistance services provided by university students on a free basis.

GLOSSARY

For ease of reference, while not a comprehensive glossary, definitions of some of the key legal terms used in this book are provided here.

accused: a person accused of a criminal offence

Act: expression of will of a parliamentary or law-making body

Act of Sederunt: delegated legislation whereby the courts may enact rules regarding court procedure

action: proceedings commenced in a civil court

adjudication: (1) a form of diligence over heritable property; (2) a special truncated form of dispute resolution in construction disputes

admonition: a sentence handed out by a criminal court that amounts to a warning

adversarialism: type of court process prevalent in Scotland, where each side presents its own case of fact and law and the court makes a decision in favour of one party

advocate: a legal professional who traditionally has rights of audience in the higher courts

Advocate General: (1) Law Officer of the Crown who is legal adviser to UK Government on issues pertaining to Scotland; (2) court official of the European Court of Justice who issues an opinion on the case at hand to the judges

Alternative Dispute Resolution (ADR): alternatives to the court process for the resolution of civil disputes and criminal cases

appeal: appealing a court or tribunal decision on either the facts, a point of law or some procedural irregularity

appellant: party making an appeal

arbiter: the party engaged to settle a dispute in arbitration

arbitration: an alternative to the court process where parties engage an arbiter to resolve a dispute

attachment: a form of diligence over moveable property in the hands of the debtor

Attorney General: Law Officer of the Crown who advises the UK Government on legal issues

award: decision given by arbiter in arbitration

bail: being released from custody pending a trial

Bar: the collective name for the advocacy profession

bicameral: a parliamentary system with two legislative houses

Bill: an expression of Parliamentary intent

Bill of Advocation: right of appeal in the criminal courts, made, on the basis of some procedural irregularity, by the prosecutor

Bill of Suspension: right of appeal in the criminal courts, made, on the basis of some procedural irregularity, by the defence

byelaw: delegated legislation passed by a local authority

case law: decisions of the courts

case-management: a process by which courts attempt to take control of, and speed up, the timetabling of different aspects of the court process

Civil law: (1) law that generally regulates relationships between private parties (ie non-criminal); (2) law which is derived historically from Roman law

codifying Act: an Act which brings into statute previous common law principles which have governed an area

(The) Commission: executive body of the EU

Common law: (1) law which has developed from non-statutory sources; (2) law that is drawn in a historical sense from English law

community service: sentence of the criminal courts whereby an offender must carry out free work in the community

complainer: victim in a criminal case

complaint: document setting out criminal charges in a summary case

consolidation Act: an Act which brings together a number of other Acts in the same place

constitutional convention: a non-binding, customary rule of the constitution

(The) Council: main legislative body of the EU

Court of Session: Scotland's highest civil court

Court of the First Instance: court within the European Court of Justice that often deals with cases in the first instance

Court of the Lord Lyon: court dealing with heraldry, the right to bear arms and the use of clan badges

courts martial: UK-wide courts which have been established within the armed forces to deal with military disciplinary matters

criminal law: law which sets out a minimum level of societal conduct

damages: remedy provided by civil courts which amounts to financial compensation

declaratory Act: an Act designed to re-state the law, often in the aftermath of an unpopular or inconvenient court decision

decree: judgment given by a civil court

defences: statement by way of defence lodged by a defender in a civil action

defender: party defending a civil action

delegated legislation: legislation enacted where the right to legislate has been delegated by Parliament to some other person or body

devolution: the process by which powers were vested upon the Scottish Parliament from the UK Parliament

devolved areas: spheres of law in which the Scottish Parliament is competent to enact legislation

diet: a court hearing

diligence: a process by which creditors can enforce the payment of court debts by the "freezing" and sometimes sale of the debtor's assets

diligence over earnings: diligence over the earnings of the debtor

district court: lowest court in the criminal hierarchy

Employment Appeal Tribunal: body that hears appeals from employment tribunals

employment tribunal: body that settles civil disputes arising in the employment sphere

equity: process by which the law may be softened in practice in Scotland (eg by way of equitable court remedies)

European Court of Human Rights: court enforcing provisions of the European Convention on Human Rights against states who are signatories thereto

European Court of Justice: court of the European Union

European Parliament: principally an advisory body in the EC law-making process

Faculty of Advocates: governing body for advocates

fatal accident inquiry: state-mandated inquiry held in the aftermath of a fatal accident

feudalism: system of landownership in which all land vests in the Crown and is granted to other tenants in return for feu duties

feu duty: service rendered in return for granting of land

First Minister: head of the Scottish Executive

fiscal fine: financial penalty payable in minor crime instead of prosecution through the courts

formal source: source of law which renders a particular legal rule binding

full bench: a sitting of the High Court of Justiciary consisting of more than the minimum number of judges required to hear an appeal

(action of) furthcoming: a procedure by which items subject to diligence may be brought to auction and sold

golden rule: rule of statutory interpretation where courts will interpret statutes in a literal fashion except where this would give rise to an absurd result

Green Paper: government expression of legislative intent issued for consultation

hereditary peer: member of the House of Lords by virtue of historical birth-right

High Court of Justiciary: highest criminal court in Scotland

House of Commons: elected chamber of UK Parliament

House of Lords: (1) non-elected, second Chamber of UK Parliament; (2) judicial committee of House of Lords is highest civil court in the UK

indictment: document setting out criminal charges that an accused will face under solemn procedure

inhibition: a form of diligence over heritable property

Inner House: the appeal court within the Court of Session

institutional writer: eminent legal jurist whose writings became regarded as a valid formal source of law

interdict: civil court decree which prohibits a party from taking some course of action

interim interdict: civil court decree which prohibits a party from taking some course of action pending full resolution of the case

judicial precedent: process by which court decisions become binding on subsequent ones

judicial review: process by which action of public bodies can be reviewed in the court

junior counsel: a lower-ranked advocate who is not yet a QC (senior counsel)

jury: members of the public who determine the facts of cases in both criminal and (rarely) civil cases

justiciars: historical judicial figures who represented the Crown

justice of the peace: non-legally qualified judge in district courts

Lands Tribunal for Scotland: tribunal with a statutory power to deal with various types of dispute involving land or property

Lands Valuation Appeal Court: court that hears appeals from decisions of local valuation appeal committees and the Scottish Lands Tribunal

Law Society of Scotland: regulatory body for solicitors

lawyer: a general term for a legal professional

lay: denotes that a party is not legally qualified

legal aid: state financial assistance for the provision of legal advice, assistance and representation

liberal rule: rule of statutory interpretation in which statutes are interpreted in a liberal way to afford them the meaning that Parliament is taken to have intended

life peer: appointed member of the House of Lords

literal rule: rule of statutory interpretation in which statutes are interpreted in a strict, to the letter, fashion

litigation: civil court proceedings

Lord Advocate: head of prosecution service in Scotland and member of the Scottish Executive

Lord Justice-Clerk: depute to Lord President (and Lord Justice-General) in Scotland's superior courts

Lord Justice-General: head judge in the High Court of Justiciary (same person as Lord President)

Lord Ordinary: judge in the Outer House of the Court of Session

Lord President: Scotland's senior judge (heads both High Court of Justiciary and Court of Session)

Lords of Appeal in Ordinary: judges who sit in the Judicial Committee of the House of Lords

Lords of Session: judges in the Inner House of the Court of Session

lords superior: under the feudal system, noblemen who received land directly from a Crown grant

mediation: process by which parties may resolve their dispute with the assistance of a neutral third party

mediator: neutral third party in mediation

messenger-at-arms: executes criminal and civil processes (including diligence) in the Court of Session and High Court of Justiciary

mischief rule: rule of statutory interpretation in which statutes are interpreted in a liberal fashion to ensure that the Act deals with the legal issue it was enacted to resolve

nobile officium: equitable power of the High Court of Justiciary and Court of Session to provide remedies where the law does not provide one

obiter dicta: judicial comments in a court judgment not directly relevant to resolution of the case. These are never binding in subsequent cases

ombudsman: official who may investigate public complaints in both the public and private sectors

ordinary cause: civil court procedure in the sheriff court for actions involving more than £1,500

Outer House: the court of first instance within the Court of Session

oversman: party appointed to give award in arbitration where the two arbiters appointed by the parties cannot agree

petition: (1) process by which a party may petition a civil court for a remedy; (2) document which sets out initial charges and commences criminal proceedings in solemn procedure

petitioner: party bringing a petition in the civil courts

plea in bar of trial: a preliminary plea brought prior to the trial diet in criminal matters

pleadings: legal arguments lodged in court in a civil action

precognition: interview of witnesses in a criminal case by either the prosecution or defence

Presiding Officer: official in Scottish Parliament whose remit is to ensure the effective and lawful nature of business in the House

Private Bill: a Bill promoted by individuals or groups that are generally seeking some sort of benefit for themselves

private law: law which pertains to relations between private parties (rather than the state)

Private Member's Bill: a Bill brought by a Member of Parliament who is not a member of the Government

Privy Council: judicial committee of the Privy Council; comprises Law Lords who may hear appeals in criminal matters on devolution matters only

probation: a criminal sentence imposed by the court that amounts to a good behaviour bond

procurator fiscal: responsible for prosecuting offenders on a local basis

Public Bill: Bill which will apply to the nation in general (ie general Acts of Parliament derive from Public Bills)

public defenders: state-employed lawyers who provide legal assistance and representation for accused persons who cannot afford their own lawyers

public law: law which pertains to the relationship of the state with members of the public

pursuer: the party raising a civil action against another

QC: Queen's Counsel; a senior advocate

ratio decidendi: the rationale that was central to the decision in a previous case which may become binding in subsequent cases

record: the statement of legal arguments and responses by the parties lodged in court in a civil action. While adjustments by the parties are being made the record is said to be "open"; when the adjustments are finalised, the record is "closed"

respondent: successful party in a civil action where the other party is appealing

Restrictive Practices Court: UK-wide court that hears cases relating to monopolies, unfair pricing practices and price maintenance agreements

right of way: right of access over land which can arise by usage over time

rights of audience: rights to appear and represent parties in court

Royal Assent: monarch's "rubber-stamping" of Acts of Parliament

Scottish Law Commission: body that examines areas of law on behalf of Government

senior counsel: a senior advocate (QC)

sheriff: judge in the sheriff court

sheriff-clerk: civil servant who provides clerical assistance to sheriff

sheriff court: court with wide civil and criminal jurisdiction

sheriffdom: area in which sheriff principal exercises jurisdiction

sheriff officer: executes criminal and civil processes (including diligence) in the sheriff court

sheriff principal: head sheriff in sheriffdom; hears appeals from sheriffs in civil matters

small claim: truncated civil court procedure in sheriff court, dealing with cases where the amount of claim is below £750

solicitor: general practitioner of the law

solicitor-advocate: solicitor who has obtained extended rights of audience to appear in the superior courts in Scotland

Solicitor General: depute to the Lord Advocate

special defence: technical defences that can be mounted by an accused: insanity, incrimination, alibi and self-defence

specific implement: civil court remedy in which party is ordered to do something

stare decisis: standing by (court) decisions

stated case: appeal procedure by which the judge at first instance must state the grounds for his or her decision, which may then be reviewed by the appeal court

statutory instrument: delegated legislation made by a Government Minister

statutory interpretation: process by which a court (or lawyer) interprets legislation and applies it to a given set of facts

statutory law: law which is derived from legislation

stipendiary magistrate: judge in district courts in Glasgow

summary cause: form of civil court procedure in sheriff court where value of dispute is between £750 and £1,500

summary procedure: procedure for minor criminal offences in either the district or sheriff court (there is no jury in summary cases)

tribunal: forum in which certain civil disputes can be resolved as an alternative to the court process

unicameral: a parliamentary system in which there is only one legislative chamber

vassal: recipient of land from a lord superior under the feudal system

White Paper: government expression of parliamentary intent published for public consultation

FURTHER READING

Chapter 1

Meston and Sellar, *The Scottish Legal Tradition* (1991)

The Laws of Scotland: Stair Memorial Encyclopaedia, vol 22, "Sources of Law"

Walker, *A Legal History of Scotland,* vols 1–5 (1988–98)

Chapter 2

Ashton and Finch, *Constitutional Law in Scotland* (2000)

Ashton and Finch *Administrative Law in Scotland* (2001)

Butterworths Core Text: European Union Law (5th edn, 2008)

Buxton, "The Human Rights Act and Private Law" (2000) 116 LQR 48

Gloag and Henderson, *The Law of Scotland* (10th edn, 1995)

Himsworth and O'Neill, *Constitutional Law in Scotland* (2003)

Himsworth and O'Neill, *Scotland's Constitution: Law and Practice* (2004)

The Laws of Scotland: Stair Memorial Encyclopaedia, vol 22, "Sources of Law (Formal)"

McFadden and Lazarowicz, *The Scottish Parliament: An Introduction* (3rd edn, 2003)

Paterson, Bates and Poustie, *The Legal System of Scotland: Cases and Materials* (4th edn, 1999)

Reed and Murdoch, *A Guide to Human Rights Law in Scotland* (2nd edn, 2008)

Starmer, "Two years of the Human Rights Act" (2003) 1 EHRLR 14

Walker, *The Scottish Legal System* (8th edn, 2001)

Wade, "The United Kingdom's Bill of Rights" in Hare and Forsyth (eds), *Constitutional Reform in the UK: Practice and Principles* (1998)

White and Willock, *The Scottish Legal System* (4th edn, 2007)

Chapter 3

Auchie, *Summary Cause Procedure in the Sheriff Court* (2nd edn, 2004)

Brown, *Criminal Evidence and Procedure: An Introduction* (2nd edn, 2001)

Gloag and Henderson, *The Law of Scotland* (12th edn, 2001)

Gretton, "Striking the Balance: Warrant Sales: At the Turning Point", 2001 SLT (News) 30, 255–58

Kelbie, *Small Claims Procedure in the Sheriff Court* (1994)

The Laws of Scotland: Stair Memorial Encyclopaedia, vol 6, "Courts and Competency", "The House of Lords", "The High Court of Justiciary", "The Court of Session", "The Sheriff Court" and "The District Court"

MacPherson, "Warrant Sales: At the Turning Point", 2001 SLT (News) 35, 289–92

Paterson, Bates and Poustie, *The Legal System of Scotland: Cases and Materials* (4th edn, 1999)

White and Willock, *The Scottish Legal System* (4th edn, 2007)

Chapter 4

Clark, "Institutionalising Mediation" 2008 JR 193

Davidson, *Arbitration* (2000)

Davidson, "Some thoughts on the Draft Arbitration (Scotland) Bill" 2009 JBL 44

Hunter, *The Law of Arbitration in Scotland* (2nd edn, 2002)

Kearney, *Children's Hearings and the Sheriff Court* (2nd edn, 2000)

Macauley, "Adjudication: Rough Justice?" 2000 SLT (News) 217

McIvor et al, *Establishing Drug Courts in Scotland: Early Experiences of the Pilot Drug Courts in Glasgow and Fife* (Scottish Executive Research Report, 2003)

Malcolm and O'Donnell, *A Guide to Mediating in Scotland* (2009)

Mays and Clark, *Alternative Dispute Resolution in Scotland* (Scottish Office Central Research Unit Report, 1999)

Moody and Mackay (eds), *Greens Guide to Alternative Dispute Resolution in Scotland* (1995)

Norrie, *Children's Hearings in Scotland* (2nd edn, 2005)

Norrie, "Human Rights Challenges to the Children's Hearing System" (2000) 4 JLSS 8

Samuel, *Supporting Court Users: The In-court Advice and Mediation Projects in Edinburgh Sherif Court* (Scottish Executive Report (phase 2), 2002)

Scottish Legal Action Group, "Civil justice reform: modernising the civil justice system in Scotland" (2005) 331 SCOLAG 101

Chapter 5

MacQueen, *Studying Scots Law* (3rd edn, 2004)

The Laws of Scotland: Stair Memorial Encyclopaedia, vol 13, "Legal Profession, Solicitors" and "The Modern Faculty of Advocates"

Walker, *The Scottish Legal System* (8th edn, 2001)

Chapter 6

Goriely *et al*, *The Public Defence Solicitors' Office in Edinburgh: an independent evaluation* (Scottish Executive Central Research Unit Report, 2001)

Scottish Legal Aid Board, *The Scottish Legal Aid Board Handbooks*, available on-line at http://www.slab.org.uk/profession/handbook/index.htm

Glossary

S O'Rourke and A Duncan, *Glossary of Scottish Legal Terms* (4th edn, 2004)

INDEX